You Can SHARE the Love of GOD With Others

The Awakening Christian Series BOOK THREE

SALLIE DAWKINS

You Can Share the Love of God With Others

Book Three of The Awakening Christian Series

Copyright © 2021 by Sallie Dawkins

Published by
Firebrand United, LLC
P.O. Box 2506
Danville, Kentucky
40423-2506 USA
www.FirebrandUnited.com

Names: Dawkins, Sallie, author.

Title: You can share the love of God with others / by Sallie Dawkins.

Series: The Awakening Christian Series

Description: Includes bibliographical references. | Danville, KY: Firebrand United, LLC, 2021.

Identifiers: LCCN: 2021913943 | ISBN: 978–1–955861–04–5 (paperback) | 978–1–955861–05–2 (ebook) | 978–1–955861–13–7 (hardback) | 978–1–955861–29–8 (audio book) | 978-1-955861-32-8 (large print paperback)

Subjects: LCSH Presence of God. | Christian life. | Evangelistic work. | Interpersonal relations—Religious aspects—Christianity. | BISAC RELIGION / Christian Living / Inspirational | RELIGION / Christian Living / Personal Growth | RELIGION / Christian Living / Spiritual Growth

Classification: LCC BT121.3 .D39 2021 | DDC 231.7—dc23

Reviews

As someone who has read the first two books in The Awakening Christian Series, this one is the icing on the cake and is a must-read for fans and followers of Dawkins and her brand of Christian living. For an uplifting and heartfelt call to spiritual action in your daily life, let *You Can Share the Love of God With Others* by Sallie Dawkins be your newest Christian Resource. - Tammy R, Readers' Favorite, 5/5 Stars

Many Christians have begun to wake up to the knowledge that their spiritual life is suffering; it almost feels anemic. They've forgotten how to live God's word, to act in faith, believe in miracles, and trust their heavenly Father to provide, support, and care for them. *You Can Share the Love of God With Others* takes the reader even further into manifesting God's miracles through faith and being attentive to his urgings. I appreciate how Ms. Dawkins reveals what's missing so desperately from the Church - the spiritual side of Christianity. – Five Star Review from Susan S. for Readers' Favorite

I dedicate this book to Holy Spirit, the encouraging One. Your glorious presence and power are undeniably brilliant. Thank You for teaching me Your ways and making me laugh. You are my Comforter, Counselor, and Friend. I will love You always.

I have not kept the good news of your justice hidden in my heart; I have talked about your faithfulness and saving power. I have told everyone in the great assembly of your unfailing love and faithfulness. (Psalm 40:10 NLT)

I've chosen to obey your truth and walk in the splendor-light of all that you teach me. (Psalm 119:30 TPT)

You Can Share the Love of God With Others

Introduction

One Body with Christ as the Head

Can every Christian access God's healing power, or is this reserved for an elite few in the Body of Christ? Aren't miracles, signs, and wonders reserved for pastors and evangelists who have worldwide ministries? I assumed that's the way it was—until I discovered the truth.

If you're new to this series, you may not know my history. I was a Christian for twenty-four years when God confronted me. It was just a few days before my fiftieth birthday. *How many years would I sit on that fence of unbelief and disbelief?* The Lord asked me if I was ever going to believe He is who He says He is. My answer to Him was yes, but I admitted I didn't know Him at all. The response shocked only one of us —and it wasn't God.

The Lord didn't back down when I asked Him to teach me who He is. Instead, He responded by insisting I also needed to believe that I am who He says I am. It's been a life-altering roller-coaster ride experience ever since!

I wrote this book series for Christians seeking a closer relationship with God. Within these pages, you'll find my testimony of transformation. Under the Lord's guidance and instruction, I have undergone rapid spiritual growth in the brief span of five years. Just as in the previous books in the series, I encourage readers to confront assumptions, doubts, and beliefs. Oh, and to be clear, all God's children are special to Him (Isaiah 43:4 TLB), and I believe all born-again, Spirit-filled Christians can access His healing power.

Jesus commissioned His disciples to go into the world to preach the gospel. He also granted them authority to place their hands on the sick to see them healed (Mark 16:18 TLB). The gift of healing is plural—it's *gifts of healings* (1 Corinthians 12:9 NKJV). Our healing comes in many different ways. As Christ's disciples, we also received His commission. We're *sent ones* who go into the world to make more disciples.

To receive the gift of salvation, we had to believe it was for us (Mark 16:16 TLB). We receive the gift of tongues in the same way. Is healing also received by faith? Suppose we think that God's healing miracles expired when Jesus died. In that case, we might not see anyone healed or have faith to believe that our prayers are powerful enough to minister healing to others.

However, if we believe the Bible is the eternal living Word of God and that Christ's words are literal, we will believe healing comes when we place our hands on the sick. That's a very different mindset, isn't it? Why, then, do we see so few Christians operating in the gifts of healings? You'll find answers to these questions and more in the pages of this book!

2

God is Always Speaking

Once we grasp our true identity in Christ, everything changes. As born-again, Spirit-filled believers in Christ, we're naturally supernatural! We're new creations (2 Corinthians 5:17), and we believe that nothing in life happens apart from God.

With that perspective, I see God in all things. I choose to use heavenly frames and lenses to view this world. It's a choice I first had to make intentionally, and part of the testimony I shared in book two of this series. I believe, as disciples of Christ, we can learn from everything around us. The following story illustrates this point well.

The Lord used a recent shoulder issue to increase my awareness of His Body's need to be strengthened. For over a year, I prayed consistently for healing of my left shoulder. There was no trauma or injury that I could recall. Still, the range of motion gradually decreased, and a nagging pain set in. It was beyond annoying.

When problems first started, I was sure they weren't mine. It wasn't normal for my body. In Jesus' name, I commanded the pain to go and declared total healing according to God's word (Matthew 8:7 NKJV). Though the pain wasn't from God, I considered perhaps God was using this affliction to increase my awareness and compassion for others. Over the next year, I was fascinated by how many Christians I encountered with shoulder pain or a frozen shoulder. I prayed for many to be healed and saw miraculous results. Still, the muscles in my shoulder and arm were not quite right. Jesus was moved with compassion to pray for others (Mark 1:41 NKJV), but He didn't walk around in physical pain.

God speaks to us in many ways. One of the fun ways He communicates with me is through idioms. Idioms are figures of speech not meant to be taken literally, but that's not always the case when God shares them. It was a moment of deep conviction when the Lord lovingly pointed out that I was *trying to do things single-handedly.* I allowed my right shoulder to carry all the burden. Shoulders often symbolize strength to carry responsibility (Isaiah 9:6). However, it's not God's will for us to do things in our own power and strength (2 Corinthians 12:9–10).

My right arm carried all the weight, and my left arm was *going along for the ride.* My left shoulder restriction threw my entire body out of alignment as compensations were made for the weakness. The ongoing pain started affecting other areas. *Was this a test to determine how I might respond?*

Was I going to hate my arm, disown it, amputate it, or talk bad about it to others? No! The love and care that we extend to our own bodies should be the same care we offer to the Body of Christ—but is it? *Was the Lord using this to reveal an opportunity for growth in my life?*

My arm had potential, and I wanted to help it, but I didn't know how. That's why, eventually, I mentioned the issue to my health care provider. I tried every other thing I knew to do. I needed help from a specialist. *Was my shoulder pain about the Body learning to work together?* I was still asking God for clarity.

Thankfully, physical therapists are pros at helping people recover from muscle loss. After the initial assessment, I received several straightforward exercises designed to help regain lost strength. The remedy was uncomplicated and proved to be very helpful. Where my right arm and shoulder had been doing all the heavy lifting, now my left arm and shoulder were gradually re-engaging. Strength and range of motion increased in just a few weeks!

Did I question God's love when my shoulder wasn't instantly healed? Did I make excuses for why the Lord didn't heal my shoulder? Did I say, "Well, this is just one of those things that the Lord is going to have to work out, and I know it takes time"? No!

I'm so glad God's word is clear in 1 Corinthians 12 that there are many varied gifts of healings and that He left me with options. Did it show a lack of faith to consult a doctor when I know God is my Healer? I don't believe it did. God wants us to prosper and be in good health (3 John 2 NKJV), and He often uses others to help us through the process.

I'm grateful that the Lord's mercies are new every day (Lamentations 3:22-23). While physical therapy helped tremendously, about six months later, I was still experiencing intermittent pain. Early one Saturday morning, as I lay in bed talking with the Lord, His healing presence showed up dramatically. I wasn't thinking about my shoulder at all—but God was! It felt as if He moved me from the present and sent me back in time. I was suddenly reliving a long-buried memory.

When I was eighteen years old, I juggled working four different minimum wage jobs to make ends meet. It was a busy time! One evening, I drove through downtown Meridian, Mississippi, on my way to work. I stopped at a red light. When the signal turned green, I pulled forward. A car coming off the overpass to my left ran the red light. I didn't see the car speeding toward me until just before impact.

Closing my eyes tight, I braced myself for the inevitable collision. The fast-moving vehicle crashed into my car with enough force to total the vehicle. The vision was so real that it startled me afresh thirty-seven years later. I not only heard the impact but also felt it. I experienced an unexpectedly violent response as muscle memory of that trauma was released. A sudden loud POP! and instantly, my shoulder realigned. All pain was gone. A more significant measure of healing had gloriously taken place!

Although I couldn't recall any specific injuries that might have caused my shoulder to hurt, God had not forgotten. I had prayed many times for the Lord to reveal to me what was going on. I never expected that God would answer my prayers in this way. I laughed and praised the Lord! Quickly dressing, I raced downstairs to share the good news with a visiting missionary and recounted the miracle that had just taken place!

The Process

From the onset, I took the matter straight to God and prayed fervently for His healing. I asked the Lord to open my spiritual eyes to see what was involved. When I went to the altar at church to request prayer for my shoulder's healing, there was a slight improvement, but it was neither total nor complete. God didn't heal my shoulder instantly, but He allowed me to partner with Him in the finished work.

Throughout the ordeal, the Lord had a lot to say about His Body, and He used my body to communicate this message to me (1 Corinthians 12:8). I persistently prayed and declared complete restoration to my body and also to the Body of Christ. The Lord often invites us to intercede in prayer for others, and I sensed Him leading me to pray for His Body to be strengthened (Romans 12:4–5, Colossians 2:19).

> The eye cannot say to the hand, "I don't need you!" And the head cannot say to the foot, "I don't need you!" No! Those parts of the body that seem to be weaker are really very important. And the parts of the body that we think are not worth much are the parts that we give the most care to. And we give special care to the parts of the body that we want to hide. The more beautiful parts of our body need no special care. But God put the body together and gave more honor to the parts that need it. God did this so that our body

would not be divided. God wanted
the different parts to care the same
for each other. If one part of the
body suffers, then all the other parts
suffer with it. Or if one part of our
body is honored, then all the other
parts share its honor. All of you
together are the body of Christ. Each
one of you is a part of that body. (1
Corinthians 12:21–27 ICB)

The pain and discomfort I felt were not from God; however, I
believe the Lord worked this issue into something good. It
had been a long time since my prayers failed to produce
immediate healing. The Lord encouraged me to keep praying.
In Mark 8:22–26, we learn that Jesus prayed for a blind man
twice. Jesus could have healed the man completely with one
prayer. Still, I believe He was teaching His disciples an
important lesson in perseverance.

Jesus took the blind man by the hand
and led him out of the village, and
spat upon his eyes, and laid his
hands over them. "Can you see
anything now?" Jesus asked him.
The man looked around. "Yes!" he
said, "I see men! But I can't see them

> very clearly; they look like tree
> trunks walking around!" Then Jesus
> placed his hands over the man's eyes
> again and as the man stared intently,
> his sight was completely restored,
> and he saw everything clearly,
> drinking in the sights around him.
> (Mark 8:23–25 TLB)

I'm grateful for this scripture because it shows us it's okay to keep on praying for healing. When our prayers are not answered immediately, will we give up or continue praying? We grow in character that strengthens our faith if we persist in prayer and believe for God's miracles to manifest.

The scripture in Mark 8:23 also teaches us that clarity of vision comes in stages. We may have insights into situations or circumstances—to see in part—and still not grasp the fuller breadth or depth of God's perspective in the matter. I believe the Lord was using my shoulder issue to invite me to pray bigger.

> This is the boldness which we have
> toward him, that if we ask anything
> according to his will, he listens to us.
> And if we know that he listens to us,
> whatever we ask, we know that we

have the petitions which we have asked of him. (1 John 5:14–15 WEB)

I didn't always know how to pray—even now, I'm no expert. I'm still learning from God in this area. Have you ever asked the Lord to teach you how to pray, or how He would have you to pray over a situation so that your words align with His?

Pray Bigger

Would you be interested in knowing the super-simple way God taught me to pray bigger and more effectively? God encouraged me to substitute the pronouns in prayers that I was already praying! By exchanging the *I, me, my, mine* pronouns with *us, we, our, His,* or *Your,* my prayers were more effective and far-reaching!

Instead of praying for *my* body, family, or children, the Lord invited me to pray for *His* Body, *His* family, and *His* children. It wasn't just my left shoulder God wanted to heal. I believe He was inviting me to join Him in praying for the entire Body of Christ to be strengthened, recovered, and restored. Only one part of the Body has greater significance than the other parts, and that's Jesus, the Head!

According to scripture, every member is vital and plays an essential role in the Body's proper functioning (Romans 12:4). When one member suffers, all the members suffer with it (1 Corinthians 12:26 NKJV). Other members of the Body of Christ are counting on us to know our roles and functions.

Together, we're growing and learning to operate efficiently and in harmony with others. The children of God are part of one family. Created in God's image and likeness, when we pray for others to be blessed, we are essentially speaking those blessings to the Lord Himself (James 3:9–10).

When the Lord draws my attention to an area of correction, these adjustments come to my life first. Then the Lord invites me to pray with and for others for similar breakthroughs. Indeed, it's the Lord who prepares us to sit with Him on the throne (Ephesians 2:4–8, 10). God is waking the sleeping Church in this era. He does not want us to stay in a place of frustration, weakness, or reluctance to ask for help—and we don't have to! He has answers. The Lord is our help in time of need (Hebrews 4:16 NKJV). He has a plan for restoring strength to every atrophied muscle in His Body. I believe that even now, Christians everywhere are awakening to their true identity and authority in Christ. What an exciting time to be alive in Christ!

Perhaps more than anything, the ongoing shoulder issue was a reminder that apart from God, I can do nothing (John 15:5). United with Christ as one, He is still actively working out the folly of self-will within me that occasionally rises against Him (Genesis 32:24–28). The Lord conquers us with an inward power (1 Corinthians 4:20), and I believe God's victories are first internal and then manifested outwardly. He is far more interested in our eternal spirit than He is our flesh.

Series Overview

This is the third and final book in *The Awakening Christian Series*. At some point in my faith walk, I got lost. Foundational truths got twisted, and I forgot what salvation was all about. Perhaps I hadn't experienced a true conversion at all.

Although *You Can Share the Love of God With Others* begins where the second book ends, it is possible to read this one and understand its message without reading the other books in the series. However, if you have not read the preceding books, some of the material may seem disconnected since the series progresses in its scriptural foundations. Books one and two focus on recognizing God's voice and heart as we grow in our relationship with Him.

Book one, *You Can Hear the Voice of God Through All Your Spiritual Senses,* answered questions that many Christians feel they can't ask in church. The enemy's lies deceived me for too long. It left me feeling lost, frustrated, defeated, and powerless. This series goes back to basics to uncover and untangle lies of the enemy that cause some Christians to falter. Asking God questions helped me grow in relationship with Him, and embracing His truths drew me out of a decades-long identity crisis.

In book two, *You Can Know the Heart of God For Your Life,* the journey of spiritual transformation continued. As my focus shifted from self toward God, my perceptions also changed. I believe this reconnection was the catalyst for supernatural spiritual growth (John 15:4–5 NKJV). Christianity is a covenant relationship with the Most High God. Jesus is the picture of what our lives can look like (Romans 8:29).

The final book, *You Can Share the Love of God With Others*, holds even greater insights. Though some of the topics included here were introduced in books one and two, the content is not duplicated. Consider it advanced course material. I believe diving deeper into these subjects will more fully prepare you for carrying out the Great Commission safely and confidently. A strong faith foundation is essential as we lead others to Christ. This book will encourage you to fulfill Jesus' Great Commission to make disciples. When Jesus was asked which command was the greatest, His response was simple.

> Jesus said to him, "'You shall love the LORD your God with all your heart, with all your soul, and with all your mind.' This is the first and great commandment. And the second is like it: 'You shall love your neighbor as yourself.' On these two commandments hang all the Law and the Prophets." (Matthew 22:37–40 NKJV)

The big picture of what we're looking at in this series is our Three-in-One Triune God—Father, Son, and Holy Spirit. We're also learning to fulfill the great command to love God with our entire being and to love others, even as we love ourselves (Mark 12:29–31 NKJV). As members of the

Church, we know the heart and voice of God and serve as the hands of Christ, asking, "How can I help you?" or "What do you want me to do for you?" (Luke 18:41 ICB).

Many within the Body of Christ seem content with casual Christianity. The days of lukewarm, half-hearted Christianity must end if our goal is to grow in spiritual maturity. If we don't know or believe that God is who He says He is, how will we ever know or receive the fullness of His love for us? And if we cannot love ourselves and who we are in Christ, how will we love others as they deserve to be loved?

In this book, you'll find more supernatural testimonies of heavenly encounters, revelations, and lessons of correction from my ongoing journey of faith. Each chapter closes with an Application Challenge, where you'll discover additional resources and questions meant to extend your learning.

I'm confident that by the end of this book, you'll find that you can share God's love with others with Holy Spirit's boldness, power, and strength. It's part of being prepared to fulfill the marching orders given to every believing Christian by our resurrected King Jesus. It's our love for Christ that compels us to move forward.

What Does God Say About This Topic?

And these attesting signs will accompany those who believe: in My name they will drive out demons; they will speak in new languages; They will pick up serpents; and [even] if they drink anything deadly, it will not hurt them; they will lay their hands on the sick, and they will get well. (Mark 16:17–18 AMPC)

Therefore we also pray always for you that our God would count you worthy of *this* calling, and fulfill all the good pleasure of *His* goodness and the work of faith with power, that the name of our Lord Jesus Christ may be glorified in you, and you in Him, according to the grace of our God and the Lord Jesus Christ. (2 Thessalonians 1:11–12 NKJV)

Let's Pray

Father God, thank You for this day and this time. You are our Great Provider. Lord, help us lay aside all self-effort and self-focus. We desire to live wholly and entirely in Your identity. Lord, forgive us for living in our own strength. We renounce all living apart from You, and we purpose to acknowledge You in all things. We desire to rest in Your strength and trust that You will work in us and through us for Your good pleasure (Ephesians 1:11).

Circumcise our hearts to live for You alone (Philippians 3:3 TPT). Lord, heal now, in Jesus' Name, every soul wound that seeks to serve self and drive a wedge between us. We desire to love You with all our heart, soul, mind, and strength (Mark 12:30 NKJV).

Spirit of Holiness, come. Fill us and possess us fully. Restore all lost time. Catch us up, Lord, to fulfill Your plans and purposes (Psalm 138:8). Pour out a fresh anointing, causing supernatural spiritual growth and maturity within Your Body. Bring us into complete alignment with Your word, Your will, and Your ways. Lord, You alone are Head over all (Colossians 2:10). We desire to live in communion with You for all our days (Psalm 27:4, 139:16 TPT).

In Jesus' Name, we declare the Body will be found fully fit, spiritually mature, and prepared to carry out all Kingdom duties with love, joy, and excellence. Thank You, Lord, for Your eternal goodness and faithfulness. Thank You for granting us access to Your glorious riches (Philippians 4:19)

—Your presence, provision, protection, and perfect health. It's in Jesus' Name we pray. Amen.

Chapter One

Work Out Your Own Salvation

Salvation is a gift we receive when we confess we are sinners in need of a Savior, and we invite Jesus to be Lord of our lives. It's a simple process, yet in my own life, it seems these concepts got twisted.

The enemy comes in and whispers lies meant to wear us down. Until suddenly (or gradually), we find we're no longer convinced of the things we were once so certain. When active Christians fail to grow spiritually, could it be a symptom pointing to a faulty faith foundation?

If you're thinking, *Wasn't my salvation worked out when I accepted Jesus as my Savior*? That's a good question, and it's one that I asked, too. *Was I absent on the day they discussed this at church?* Have you seen this verse in Philippians that directs us to work out our salvation?

Therefore, my dear ones, as you have always obeyed [my suggestions], so now, not only [with the enthusiasm you would show] in my presence but much more because I am absent, work out (cultivate, carry out to the goal, and fully complete) your own salvation with reverence *and* awe and trembling (self-distrust, with serious caution, tenderness of conscience, watchfulness against temptation, timidly shrinking from whatever might offend God and discredit the name of Christ). (Philippians 2:12 AMPC)

Many people think salvation is once and done. I've discovered that working out our salvation is a daily process because we live in a fallen world. Although we are complete in Christ at redemption, there are more spiritual blessings for us to possess. Salvation is a gift from God we progressively unwrap to receive a greater revelation of who He is. In working out our salvation, we are growing in awareness of who God is and who we are to Him.

> When someone becomes a Christian,
> he becomes a brand new person
> inside. He is not the same anymore.
> A new life has begun! (2 Corinthians
> 5:17 TLB)

Salvation belongs to those in the Body of Christ who consent and cooperate with Jesus (Ephesians 1:22–23, 5:25–30). The Lord moves to reveal Himself to us to the degree we desire Him (Jeremiah 29:13). There is a process for learning how to live out our new identity. Part of my frustration as a new Christian was when I took this *new life* verse in 2 Corinthians 5:17 literally. I thought the change would be instantaneous. That may be the case for some Christians. Still, more often than not, I believe it's a gradual process requiring an active and ongoing commitment to walking in faith and obedience daily. It's a moment-by-moment process.

Have you discovered how vital relationships are to God? Because of our sinful nature, there was no other way for us to be fully reconciled back to Father God except through the blood sacrifice of Jesus. The good news of Christ is that this sin debt is paid in full, and the righteousness of Christ now belongs to us. Jesus died *for* us and *as* us. We have been forgiven of all indebtedness, and sin no longer separates us from Father God.

As God's ambassadors, our work is the ministry of reconciliation (2 Corinthians 5:18 NKJV). This means we extend to others the same measure of forgiveness God extended to us. Leading others to salvation in Christ is part of our co-mission to expand Heaven's Kingdom on earth. Working out our salvation takes place daily for disciples of Christ.

> We are ambassadors of the Anointed
> One who carry the message of Christ
> to the world, as though God were
> tenderly pleading with them directly
> through our lips. So we tenderly
> plead with you on Christ's behalf,
> "Turn back to God and be reconciled
> to him." (2 Corinthians 5:20 TPT)

Working out our salvation means allowing God to work Christ into every part of our being—spirit, soul, and body. Allowing the Lord to touch every aspect of who we are empowers us to love the people in our lives. What if we could see it as a gift when we say, "That person brings out the worst in me!" Don't we want the worst in us to come out? The process is simple. We begin by renouncing that part of our lives that is not like God. Then, we repent of our sins and ask God to forgive our shortcomings. Finally, we invite Holy Spirit to fill all the newly vacated spaces within us with His truth and presence.

> If anyone boasts, "I love God," and
> goes right on hating his brother or
> sister, thinking nothing of it, he is a
> liar. If he won't love the person he
> can see, how can he love the God he
> can't see? The command we have
> from Christ is blunt: Loving God
> includes loving people. You've got to
> love both. (1 John 4:20–21 MSG)

Indeed, if it weren't for challenging encounters with difficult people, we might not be aware of what's within us that's not like God. Amidst these negative encounters, we're growing! We're learning to live out our new identity in Christ, but we're not doing it alone, and we're not even doing it in our own strength. Learning to maintain a Christlike attitude as we interact with others requires grace—even as the Lord lovingly reveals areas of our own lives where we're not perfectly aligned with His character yet.

> [Not in your own strength] for it is
> God Who is all the while effectually
> at work in you [energizing and
> creating in you the power and
> desire], both to will and to work for

His good pleasure *and* satisfaction
and delight. (Philippians 2:13
AMPC)

It requires our submission for God to cleanse us completely. It's our free will choice. We'll still get into Heaven without going through this process, but don't we want to be available for God's highest purposes? We belong to our Creator God as vessels, and He knows the destiny for which He created us (Acts 9:15 NKJV, James 1:18 TPT). We hold the treasure of God's truth within, and it's our honor to serve God and others. Keeping our eyes fixed on our Creator, we're changed from the inside out, and it's God helping us do it (Romans 12:1–2)!

To *work out* implies that continuous and ongoing effort is required. Although salvation has been granted to us by God through our faith in Christ, we are not yet made perfect. We are being perfected, and transformation takes place as our revelation of Christ continues to grow.

In Philippians 2:12, we're encouraged to "work out your own salvation with fear and trembling" (WEB). This word *salvation* is defined in Strong's Greek Lexicon as "welfare, prosperity, deliverance, preservation, salvation, or safety."[1] It's a continual salvation and deliverance from the molestation of enemies. Repentance connects us with salvation, but it's not a work that earns us salvation. Rather it represents a change of mind that affects our salvation.[2]

> This means that, contrary to man's perspective, the Lord is not late with his promise to return, as some measure lateness. But rather, his "delay" simply reveals his loving patience toward you, because he does not want any to perish but all to come to repentance. (2 Peter 3:9 TPT)

Repentance involves turning from sin, wrong thoughts, actions, or beliefs—or turning from fear—back to God in faith. Repentance involves a change of mind. When the eyes of our hearts are open to allow us to see the error of our ways, we repent and stop moving in the wrong direction. Sanctification is a cleansing and purifying process. We are continually working out our salvation to live holy and set apart lives dedicated fully to God.

He Gives Us a New Heart

In 1991, when I came to salvation in Christ, I had a heart of stone and knew it. I had a damaged, cold, angry, hardened heart, but God promised in Ezekiel 36:26 to give me a new, tender heart of flesh.

I will give you a new heart and put a
new spirit within you; I will take the
heart of stone out of your flesh and
give you a heart of flesh. (Ezekiel
36:26 NKJV)

In the summer of 2017, at a Friday night prayer meeting in a
little storefront church in downtown Belleville, Illinois, God
gave me that new heart. It was a life-changing encounter with
Jesus.

The continual presence of the Holy Spirit in that place was
unmistakable. It was the first place I felt safe to share what I
was sensing in the spirit realm with others. On this particular
Friday night, the Lord opened my spiritual eyes to see myself
standing in the Throne Room River of Living Water with
Jesus.

In my spirit, I heard Jesus speaking. He asked for my heart.

Yes, Lord, I quietly replied.

He waited.

*What was He waiting for? He asked for my heart, and I was
willing to give it to Him. Why was He just looking at me?*

That's when I realized Jesus was asking me to give Him my
heart, *literally*.

Is that even possible?

I glanced down to see my heart exposed. Somehow, I could see through my chest. My heart was filthy and repulsive. It was dark, filled with holes, and had strings attached to every part.

Steaming hot tears flowed down my cheeks as Jesus reached straight into my chest and grabbed hold of my tainted and broken heart.

He caressed my defiled heart like it was of great value. When God asked for my heart, He meant it.

When I said *yes*, I meant it. *But how could I live without a heart?*

I stood there, motionless, watching Jesus.

That's when He reached into His chest and removed His stunningly spotless heart. Everything about Jesus is beautiful and radiant.

Inches away, Jesus held His own heart in His hands, then gently placed His heart into my chest. I heard the *boom-boom-boom* sounds of His heart beating inside me like a drum. My pulse quickened. *Whoosh! Swoosh! Whoosh!*

A spiritual heart transplant had taken place. I felt Christ's power-infused blood coursing through my veins.

I had a deep inner knowing that my heart was God's heart, and my life was His life. It was a defining moment of realizing the extreme depths of Christ's love. Jesus willingly sacrificed everything (2 Corinthians 5:15). He withheld nothing (1 John 3:16). By example, He was inviting me to do the same.

This encounter with the Lord was real to me. Overwhelmed by His love, I walked around with my left hand resting on my chest for an entire week as if I was guarding my heart (Proverbs 4:23). I wanted nothing to come near the heart of God that would sully it.

> I have been crucified with Christ; it is no longer I who live, but Christ lives in me; and the *life* which I now live in the flesh I live by faith in the Son of God, who loved me and gave Himself for me. (Galatians 2:20 NKJV)

The heart and heartbeat of God within me were irrevocable heavenly gifts. When Jesus gave His life for us, it was so we would have eternal life with Him (John 3:16). Was this supernatural experience a reward for anything significant that I had done or said? Definitely not! I saw the filth of my heart as I stood there with Jesus. The Lord promised me a new heart through His word in Ezekiel 36:26, but it's not something I prayed for repeatedly. I surely never imagined it would happen in this unique way. This heart encounter with Jesus was a baptism of repentance for me (Acts 19:4).

If you knew you carried the literal heart of God within you, would that change your life? Would you stop listening to certain music or stop watching particular videos or movies? Would it change how you spend your time, where, or with whom? Would it change the words you speak? There was no part of my life that this encounter didn't affect.

Jesus gave me a new heart, not a restored one—and He placed this heart within me Himself. The heart of God within every Christian enables us to live in the fullness of the resurrected life of Christ, our Savior and Lord (Romans 6:5–9, 2 Corinthians 5:16–17). It's only through this God connection that we're able to live a life of love that ministers unto the Lord and moves us to extend His great love ministering to others (1 John 4:9–12 TPT).

Not only do we possess Christ's heart, but we also share in the strength of His will. Living by His example, we overcome the enemies of every Christian, namely the flesh, the world, and the devil. When Satan tempted Jesus in the wilderness, Jesus overcame him by the Word of God (1 Corinthians 10:13 NKJV, Matthew 4:1–11 NKJV). Following Christ's example, we can do the same.

This profound revelation of Christ's heart within us strengthens us to overcome the ongoing attacks of the enemy more fully. When our flesh or our enemy attempts to come against us, we overcome by clinging to Jesus—the Word of

God (Colossians 2:15). Our faith in Jesus helps us overcome the hatred of the world (John 15:18–19).

Rescued from Indecision

When I was water baptized in Christ in 1991, my new identity was in Christ. I died with Him on the cross, was buried with Him in the grave, and was resurrected into His new life as God's daughter. I was a new creation already. I was covered in the love of God and wore Christ as my righteousness. Repentance and cleansing were in that process, but somewhere along the way, I wavered in faith—I backed off from what I first believed. I wandered from the truth and sat passively on the fence of indecision for over two decades.

I *thought* I wanted God's ways for my life, but the evidence showed that part of me still wanted *my way*. My friend, I'll tell you, it's impossible to hold on to both! The only remedy is to let go of the wrong beliefs we have been holding. I shared this part of my testimony in book one of this series.

God never changes—the same is not true for us. We progressively grow into the image and likeness of God (2 Corinthians 3:18). I wrongly accepted many false labels. When healing came rapidly, it left me wondering what the authentic version of me even looked like. Would I recognize that person at all? This process stretched my beliefs, and God knew it. A vision of Jesus brought comfort.

During a time of worship, I extended my left arm heavenward. In the spirit, I saw the hand of Jesus outstretched downward toward me. I wondered if this was the same view Peter had of Jesus when he walked on water—then sank.

> So He said, "Come." And when Peter had come down out of the boat, he walked on the water to go to Jesus. But when he saw that the wind was boisterous, he was afraid; and beginning to sink he cried out, saying, "Lord, save me!" And immediately Jesus stretched out *His* hand and caught him, and said to him, "O you of little faith, why did you doubt?" (Matthew 14:29–31 NKJV)

Jesus grabbed hold of my wrist with a firm rescue hold. In my inner spirit, I heard Him clearly say, *I've got you.* The following week in worship, Jesus appeared again—just as He had before. I laughed out loud as I heard Him say, *I've still got you!* Friend, our confidence is not in our limited human strength. Our trust and faith are in our Rescuer, Jesus Christ.

Our assurance is in God's love and faithfulness. Even if we lose our grip—the Lord never will. Even if we fail Him— He'll never fail us. This vision of Jesus encouraged and strengthened me, but it also prompted me to ask Him if there were any areas of my life where I felt I was sinking. *Was there a storm of resistance in my soul preventing me from knowing Him in a more significant way? Was there an area where doubt had crept in? Was this a correction?*

The Lord might have said, *Sallie, we need to talk about some areas of unbelief in your life. Unbelief is not from Me.* But wasn't it so much sweeter the way He started that conversation? He sensed something within me I didn't sense within myself, and He was letting me know He's got a firm hold on me. If I'm looking to Jesus, I cannot fail.

> He will not let you fall. Your guardian will not fall asleep. (Psalm 121:3 GW)

God often corrects our wrong beliefs, not by focusing on the wrong, but on shifting our gaze to the strength and truth of who He is (Mark 6:5–6). When we encounter our loving God through His living word, it empowers us in magnificent ways —and it all starts with believing in Him!

A Continual Saving

In John 8:44, we learn the devil is our accuser. He is a liar and a murderer. Everything he speaks is false. Ephesians 6:12 (TPT) mentions "evil spirits that hold this dark world in bondage." When we listen to the devil's lies, we adopt wrong beliefs. These lies result in sinful thoughts, limitations, fears, unbelief, addictions, anger, hatred, jealousy, pride, and more —none of which is from God. Self-hatred counts, too. Even if we think we are not hurting anyone else, when we have self-hatred and put ourselves down, we're speaking against God's creation. We're saying God made a mistake. We aren't always aware of wrong thoughts or the impact of our words, but when we're not in complete agreement or alignment with what God says, we have sided with the enemy of our soul.

When we agree with Satan's lies, we've sided with God's enemy.

When we don't believe what God says about us, are we saying that God is wrong? If we say the redemption price that Jesus paid for us was not enough—that's a lie of the enemy. It's God's will for us to prosper in every area of life (3 John 1:2, Psalm 84:11). Suppose we have areas of life where we're not flourishing (health, finances, relationships, etc.). In that case, this might indicate that we're not aligned with God's word in those areas. All we need to do is ask Him about it. There's no reason to delay walking in the fullness of freedom God has for us (John 8:32).

When we believe the enemy's lies over the truth of God's word, it prevents us from growing in spiritual maturity. Our obedience to God allows us to receive His benefits and blessings, including His hand of protection over our lives.

> But your iniquities have separated
> you from your God; And your sins
> have hidden *His* face from you, So

that He will not hear. (Isaiah 59:2
NKJV)

God respects our free will and freedom to choose Him—or
reject Him—in every matter. He desires our willing consent
to come to Him and be filled with the power of the Holy
Spirit that enables us to walk in faith every day. When we
listen to and follow our fleshly desires instead of God, it's a
sign that the love of Christ within us has not yet been made
full (Galatians 5:6 ICB).

In our willing submission to God, we discover true freedom.
We learn obedience with every act of faith as we freely follow
Christ (Ephesians 4:24 ICB). This is *working out our
salvation,* and it requires fastening our loyalty to Christ alone.
It's this submission to God's Lordship that changes us.

What Does God Say About This Topic?

Having such great promises as these, dear friends, let us turn away from everything wrong, whether of body or spirit, and purify ourselves, living in the wholesome fear of God, giving ourselves to him alone. (2 Corinthians 7:1 TLB)

And *do* this, knowing the time, that now *it is* high time to awake out of sleep; for now our salvation *is* nearer than when we *first* believed. The night is far spent, the day is at hand. Therefore let us cast off the works of darkness, and let us put on the armor of light. (Romans 13:11–12 NKJV)

Then I heard a loud voice saying in heaven, "Now salvation, and strength, and the kingdom of our God, and the power of His Christ have come, for the accuser of our brethren, who accused them before our God day and night, has been cast down. And they overcame him by the blood of the Lamb and by the word of their testimony, and they did not love their lives to the death." (Revelation 12:10–11 NKJV)

Application Challenge

What does salvation look like in your life? What are some steps you take to work out your salvation daily?

Repentance and forgiveness are core salvation beliefs. Journal and ask, "Lord, is there anyone I need to forgive?"

How would your life be different if you knew you carried the heart of God within you?

Jesus is the only way to eternal salvation with Father God. Do you believe Christ died *for* you? Do you believe Christ died *as* you? Do you believe Christ lives *in* you? Do you believe Christ lives *through* you?

Let's Pray

Father God, in Jesus' Name, we thank You for Your faithfulness. You are faithful to complete the wonderful work You have begun in us. Thank You, Jesus, for making way for us to work out our salvation hand in hand with You. We are Yours, and we want to be fully possessed by You. Holy Spirit, thank You for teaching us how to live out our identity as ambassadors of the Kingdom of God in a way that brings You honor and glory.

Lord, thank You for the gift of salvation, which blossoms like a beautiful rose. Thank You for continually working within us to bring about complete spiritual maturity. Send Your ministering angels to minister truth to us. Remove any hindrances that prevent us from growing in our relationship with You. We yield ourselves to Your love and thank You for liberating us from the labels and lies of the enemy. Lord, we want to encounter You face-to-face. Thank You for clarity of vision, new hearts, fresh breath, and wholeness in every area. It's in the mighty Name of Jesus we pray. Amen.

Chapter Two

Sanctification

Perhaps our most significant work in salvation is to trust in God and rest in the finished work of Christ (John 19:30). Had I been confusing salvation with sanctification? A recent encounter with the Lord brought correction and encouragement! Holy Spirit has already equipped us with all we will ever need to fulfill every task the Lord sets before us (1 Corinthians 12:4–7). He reminded me He is always with me, no matter what the enemy would have me believe.

In this God encounter, the Holy Spirit presented me with a sizeable military-style duffle bag on wheels. I sensed the Lord was saying that everything I might need for carrying out the Great Commission was right there in that bag (Matthew 28:19).

In the spirit realm, I could see myself rolling that duffel bag around to different places. It was my choice to bring that bag with me. The Lord communicated that every Christian has similar access to unique gifts and tools with which God has equipped him.

Holy Spirit instructed me to open the bag. As I did, I saw it was full of tools. I reached in and grabbed hold of a tool, then extended that item toward Him for inspection. His wordless correction asked, *Really?* The Lord was encouraging me to reconsider my thoughts or beliefs about things.

There was a familiar silent dialogue between us.

I might ask, *What is this?*

He might ask, *Why do you have that?*

Some tools I pulled out of the bag were broken, which surprised me. *How did I get worthless, twisted, useless things like that in my bag?* They were not from God! It should have been obvious they were poorly constructed counterfeits. Apparently, not obvious enough.

Holy Spirit wanted to know, *Where did you get that? Who issued that to you?*

Wow! Those were good questions! Yes, there were "issues" that needed to go! Some items I retrieved from the bag went straight into the garbage. *Refuse the refuse,* the Spirit of Holiness said as He admonished me to reject all rubbish— because there's no need to hold on to worthless things (Philippians 3:8 NLT)! He questioned repeatedly, *Why are you holding on to that? Where did you get it?*

What was the point of this encounter? I believe God was teaching me how to exercise the gift of discerning of spirits. I had picked up counterfeit tools when I accepted false doctrines and perverted theology without question. I hadn't done my job to test what was being taught and compare it to the standard of truth found in scripture (1 John 4:1; Acts 17:11).

Holy Spirit let me know I already had all the tools I would ever need—if only I would use them! God was inviting me to clean out my toolbox. The good news is that He didn't make me do it alone. It's exciting to take hold of the gifts, tools, and weapons issued by God—these are beautiful, valuable resources! Why do we hold on to worthless things and attempt to carry around junk that's not from God? I needed to spend more time with God sorting through the stuff I had been shouldering.

This God encounter helped me better understand salvation and sanctification. Sanctification often happens over time, but it doesn't happen apart from God (Romans 12: 1–2). This cleansing is so important to God that He has given us special tools to help us through the daily process. He has tools and resources for each of us.

Information alone will not bring inner transformation.

One tool for sanctification is the study of God's word. If we don't know God's word, how can we know God? Knowing *about* God is good, but information alone will not bring inner transformation. Our willingness to believe and receive God's love changes the condition of our hearts. Sanctification comes in our relationship with God amid daily heart-to-heart encounters as we sit with Him face-to-face (John 17:17 NKJV).

The root of sanctification is God's love and may come through ministry and serving others. Sanctification also comes through prayer, worship, and Godly fellowship with other believers. The sanctification process empties us of all that we think we know and fills us with the fullness of God.

> Then you will be empowered to discover what every holy one experiences—the great magnitude of the astonishing love of Christ in all its dimensions. How deeply intimate and far-reaching is his love! How enduring and inclusive it is! Endless love beyond measurement that transcends our understanding—this extravagant love pours into you until you are filled to overflowing with the fullness of God! (Ephesians 3:18–19 TPT)

Being Set Free from a False Mindset

Unavoidably, we're tempted to pick up stuff as we walk through life because we hear things here and there. We may grab hold of thoughts or beliefs that aren't entirely true and accept them without question. I often feel like God corrects me more than any other human alive on the planet, so I'm grateful for the times when He allows me to learn from others.

During a 2017 healing conference in Caseyville, Illinois, Christian healing evangelist Joan Hunter asked if anyone needed new knees. A woman from the audience stood up. She juggled carrying an oxygen tank while she leaned into a walker and moved toward the front of the church. As she stood near Joan, she smiled awkwardly and asked if she could have a new heart instead of new knees. She shared she was on a transplant list for a new heart, so new knees wouldn't do her much good if she didn't get the heart. That makes sense, doesn't it? It seems logical. Except that's not how God thinks!

That way of thinking placed limitations on God and said God could do one or the other, but not *both*. Joan asked her if it would be all right if God answered her prayer for both. God intends to heal us and make us whole. Indeed, it's not too much to ask Him to provide both new knees *and* a new heart! Well, that's what they agreed upon—and you know what? This woman got a few other things, too. Within three minutes, everything changed! She removed the oxygen line, started jumping up and down, then tossed aside her walker and began running around the church praising God!

Before this event, I hadn't considered how my thoughts and views limited what God *could* or *would* do. I asked the Lord to show me any other areas where my thoughts had limited my beliefs of Him.

The devil's deceptions are often subtle, but we know he is a liar and that "sin lies" (Genesis 4:7 NKJV). The Lord warns us to guard against opening doors to sin. Satan would have us believe we are not like God and that the Lord doesn't want us to be like Him (Genesis 1:27). The sanctification process is a beautiful restoration gift from God and part of our inheritance in Christ. It's an invitation to be freed of every defilement (John 13:1–13 TPT, 1 John 1:9 TPT, Romans 6:5 TPT).

When we hear the whispers of God or feel Him gently reminding us of our past, it's never to condemn us. God is a loving Father who desires that we live in complete victory. As we purify our thoughts in the Living Water of God's word, we begin to think as Jesus thinks. The light of God's word exposes wrong thinking, critical attitudes, negative words, false beliefs, and hidden motives. The question we face then is, "What will we do with what's exposed?"

A Continual Cleansing

When we wander from God's truth and turn back to Him, will His heart grow cold toward us? Never. Every time we come to our senses and remember the truth of who we are, God's arms are open to meet us, to embrace us, to robe us in His righteousness, and to restore us fully (Luke 15:11–32). I believe God is always calling to us, beckoning us to come up higher to see as He sees. We can be intentional in asking God to check our hearts. "Lord, is there anything in my heart or in my life that doesn't please You?" Though it may feel like sanctification is sin-focused, I believe it's a beautiful gift, which reveals God's love for us. God loves us first and corrects us second!

> Search me, O God, and know my
> heart; Try me, and know my
> anxieties; And see if *there is any*
> wicked way in me, And lead me in
> the way everlasting. (Psalm 139:23–
> 24 NKJV)

Whatever the revelation-light exposes, it will also correct, and everything that reveals truth is light to the soul. This is why the Scripture says, "Arise, you sleeper! Rise up from your coffin and the Anointed One will shine his light into you!" (Ephesians 5:13–14 TPT)

What happens when the Lord brings up an issue of which we're sure we've already repented? Does that mean God hasn't forgiven our confessions of sin? No! Standing in the shower, talking with God one recent morning, I said, "Lord, wash me, and I shall be made clean."

The Lord quickly responded, *You are already clean. You only need to wash your feet.* That's a curious thing to hear, isn't it? Still, it's scriptural.

> "No," Peter protested, "you shall
> never wash my feet!" "But if I don't,
> you can't be my partner," Jesus
> replied. Simon Peter exclaimed,

"Then wash my hands and head as
well—not just my feet!" Jesus
replied, "One who has bathed all
over needs only to have his feet
washed to be entirely clean." (John
13:8–10 TLB)

When we step out to fulfill the Great Commission with Him,
God calls our feet beautiful (Romans 10:15 TLB). I believe in
this instance, the Lord was speaking to me about the
sanctification process. Because the disciples walked
everywhere, their feet were covered in dirt and filth. The
blood of Jesus washes us and makes us clean (Hebrews
10:21–22), but as we walk through the world, our feet get
dirty. Our feet require washing, and Jesus isn't asking us to
wash our feet apart from Him. He's inviting us to trust that
our souls (and the soles of our feet) will be made clean in His
holy hands. We can't hide anything from God, and apart from
Him, we can do nothing.

When we confess our sins to Christ and ask His forgiveness,
we receive, by faith, the cleansing power of His blood (Acts
15:9, 1 John 1:7–9). He cleanses not only our feet but also our
conscience. Psalm 51:7 TPT says it this way, "Wash me in
your love until I am pure in heart."

No one can see all his own mistakes.
Forgive me for my secret sins. Keep
me from the sins that I want to do.
Don't let them rule me. Then I can be
pure and free from the greatest of
sins. I hope my words and thoughts
please you. Lord, you are my Rock,
the one who saves me. (Psalm
19:12–14 ICB)

God forgives when we are intentional about turning from our sins. God knows our heart's motives, but it seems there are many layers to some of our wrong beliefs. God reveals every layer at just the right time and in just the proper order to ensure that we achieve complete victory and lasting healing.

Night Vision: "Get This Off Your Chest"

The Lord often sends His angels to minister healing and creative miracles in our lives. No two encounters or experiences are ever the same. One evening, I felt like I was part of a real-life Operation board game as I awakened from sleep to find angels standing over me.

They had cut my chest wide open. A spiritual surgery was taking place, yet there was no pain. All my internal organs were exposed. The Lord was overseeing it and guiding the angels through the process.

I could hear their unspoken words.

She needs to get this off her chest.

This needs to be removed.

This has to come out.

This is causing a blockage.

This is not supposed to be here.

These heavenly hosts were removing a lot of things—but what were they exactly? I believe the Lord was revealing that I had internalized false or counterfeit words that weren't good to have or hold. Our Lord plants good seeds, but the enemy plants poisonous weeds (Matthew 13:24-30 TPT). These bad seeds had taken root and started causing significant obstructions. These hindrances affected the proper functioning of everything within me. It clogged my internal systems with labels.

Labels? Yes, and written upon those labels were harsh words! This was not God's perfect plan for my life. Jesus, our Great Physician (Mark 2:17), took steps to remove every cancerous growth, tumor, tag, label, and restriction within me to bring healing to my life.

In Jeremiah 31:33 (NKJV) we read, "But this *is* the covenant that I will make with the house of Israel after those days, says the LORD: I will put My law in their minds, and write it on their hearts; and I will be their God, and they shall be My people." The NKJV footnote for this text clarifies that the word *heart* here literally means "inward parts." Our authentic and best life only comes from a genuine heart connection with God. Without this heart connection, our plans and actions are futile. What fruit can we bear independent of the True Vine (John 15:1 NKJV)? Christ asks us to partner with Him in this work for our benefit, growth, and maturity. Jesus needed to grow in wisdom and maturity (Luke 2:52). How much more do we also need to grow in faith?

As we confront these strongholds, lies, and wrong beliefs, we change our minds and decide to go a different way—God's way. We are co-laboring with God to purge ourselves of all that is not like Him. That's what the sanctification process is all about. As we grow in spiritual maturity, we are continually advancing and moving forward to lay hold of every promise of God. It's an inward transformation of holiness that empowers us to live a beautiful life that honors God.

What Does God Say About This Topic?

Now, may the God of peace and harmony set you apart, making you completely holy. And may your entire being—spirit, soul, and body—be kept completely flawless in the appearing of our Lord Jesus, the Anointed One. The one who calls you by name is trustworthy and will thoroughly complete his work in you. (1 Thessalonians 5:23–24 TPT)

I know that whatever God does, it endures forever; nothing can be added to it nor anything taken from it. And God does it so that men will [reverently] fear Him [revere and worship Him, knowing that He is]. (Ecclesiastes 3:14 AMPC)

Application Challenge

Read Colossians 2:15. The devil is under our feet and doesn't have a right to whisper in our ears. God is bigger than any of our blocks, issues, or baggage. Journal and ask, "Lord, am I holding on to anything not issued by You?" If so, where did this "issue" come from? Is it beneficial to keep holding on to it, or would it be better to discard it?

Internal negative patterns and cycles limit who God means for us to be. Journal and ask, "Father God, how do You see me?"

What labels are you wearing? For what are you known? God's love expresses itself uniquely through you and your gifts. How does this look in your life?

Let's Pray

Lord God, we welcome Your Triune presence in our lives. We ask for wisdom as we purpose to live holy and set apart lives that honor You. Holy Spirit, we ask You to help us fulfill this purpose in our lives. Lord, we believe that You have already completed the works of salvation and sanctification within us, and we thank You for a greater revelation of Your love for us.

Indeed, we cannot do anything apart from You—forgive us for trying. Thank You for Your equipping gifts that empower us to accomplish all You have called us to do. We pour out our praise to You alone. It's in the mighty Name of Jesus we pray. Amen.

Chapter Three

Call on Jesus

Who is this girl? And who's her daddy?

Those were the questions running through my mind after a random God encounter one summer evening in 2018.

I was walking on a rural trail with my dog at my side. Coming from the opposite direction, exiting the path, was a young teenage girl and her dog. I didn't recognize this girl, but she walked right up to me and said, "The trail has overgrown too much to run on. I told my daddy about it, and he's going to make a call to someone to get it cut."

This young girl spoke with confidence and assurance in her father's authority. She was speaking of her earthly father, of course, but at that moment, the Lord used this meeting to challenge my beliefs of Him.

This teen was deliberate in what she said. It wasn't so much what she said as how she said it that caught my attention. She hadn't stopped to have a conversation. She simply relayed the information and kept right on moving.

Holy Spirit was in this encounter. I pondered the girl's words as I walked. I blurted out, "Who was that?" My dog didn't answer, and the Lord was silent, too. That's when I thought, *Who's her daddy?* She said, "I called my daddy...," and she had every confidence that he would take care of the issue. Her daddy must have been someone with influence. An overgrown trail is a minor hindrance in the grand scheme of things, but it was important to this girl. She knew her father had the power to get things done, and she had called him immediately from right there on the trail. She noticed something out of place, and she handed the matter straight over to her father, fully confident that he would take care of it. Then she let me know. She didn't know me. I was just the next person on the trail.

She wasn't dwelling on it or worried about it. She wasn't whining or complaining about it. She saw a need, communicated it immediately to her father, and then relayed that message to the very next person she met. That was the entire encounter.

My friend, this girl was a daughter who relied on her human father to help her. How much more then can we, as children of God—princes and princesses—go to our Father the King and ask Him to take care of things?

> Don't bargain with God. Be direct.
> Ask for what you need. This isn't a
> cat-and-mouse, hide-and-seek game
> we're in. If your child asks for bread,

do you trick him with sawdust? If he asks for fish, do you scare him with a live snake on his plate? As bad as you are, you wouldn't think of such a thing. You're at least decent to your own children. So don't you think the God who conceived you in love will be even better? (Matthew 7:7–11 MSG)

The Lord knows the desires of our hearts. This girl's earthly daddy knew his daughter enjoyed jogging with her dog. Our heavenly Father knows what we like, too. Even more so! This encounter challenged me to ask the Lord to reveal areas where I wasn't fully trusting Him. Did I think some things were too small—or too big—for Him? Was I trying to solve things independently because I didn't want to bother Him—like He's too busy to answer when I call? At that moment, I didn't have answers—I had questions. The Lord was inviting me to ask Him for more. Do we believe God is far away and that it takes a long time for our prayers to reach Him? This couldn't be further from the truth!

Have I not commanded you? Be strong and of good courage; do not be afraid, nor be dismayed, for the

> LORD your God *is* with you wherever you go. (Joshua 1:9 NKJV)

> Do you not know that you are the temple of God and *that* the Spirit of God dwells in you? (1 Corinthians 3:16 NKJV)

One of the names God calls Himself is *Immanuel* which translates as "God with us" (Matthew 1:23 NKJV). He is the Great I AM (Exodus 3:14 TLB), the Sovereign and living God (Ephesians 4:6 AMPC). Each of God's names has a unique way of revealing His nature in a particular way that allows us to have a bigger, more precise picture of who He is. When we talk with God in prayer, we can call on any of His names.

Disconnected and Reconnected

God often speaks to me in visions and pictures. He has spoken to me on more than one occasion by showing me an old-fashioned telephone switchboard from the 1940s or '50s. In those days, operators manually routed calls by connecting wires into a large circuit board. Operators monitored all the conversations.

When the Lord shows me old switchboards and their operators, He may be letting me know He's making new connections. These connections might include new links with people or an expansion in the service area. At other times when I see angels serving as operators, the Lord is letting me know I can rest knowing my call or calling are secure. Still, other times, He's warning me of a poor connection.

When I call on God, I don't have to go through a switchboard operator, other people, or other channels to get to Him. I can call on Jesus directly any time of the day or night, assured that the Lord will always answer the call personally. He will never put me on hold, and I'll never get a voice recording to leave a message! While it may seem like some Christians have a direct line to heaven, the truth is, *all* Christians can have that same direct-line access.

Call to Me, and I will answer you, and show you great and mighty things, which you do not know. (Jeremiah 33:3 NKJV)

When you pray, you should go into your room and close the door. Then pray to your Father who cannot be seen. Your Father can see what is done in secret, and he will reward you. (Matthew 6:6 ICB)

There was a time in the not-so-distant past when my prayer life was limited to nonverbal, sounds-real-good-inside-my-head kinds of prayers. Then I upgraded to spoken prayers. It was a bumpy transition. These prayers were often begging-pleading, whining-complaining, and half-hearted. "Lord, if it's Your will to heal..." or "Lord, if You could do this...."

Where did I learn to pray that way? Certainly not from Jesus! Still, I believe God hears our prayers, whether unspoken or spoken (Matthew 8:5–13 NKJV, Mark 5:28 NLT). If we allow Him, He will guide us to the most effective way to pray in all our situations (Romans 8:26–27).

In a society that values self-sufficiency, self-reliance, and self-help, it's often hard to confess our needs to others or ask for help. Even after being a Christian for decades, I didn't have an I'm-fully-dependent-on-You personal kind of heart relationship with God. Everything I knew about God was all in my head, right along with a tangled mass of mixed-up thoughts and beliefs.

My views of God were limited, and so was my way of thinking. *Was He so busy He didn't have time for me? Was I an obligation and a burden to Him? If I studied more, would He love me more? When He found out how damaged and broken I was, would He regret His purchase? If I called Him, would He answer?*

What Does It Mean to "Call on the Name of Jesus"?

Outside of a personal relationship with the Lord, we might reserve calling on Jesus for emergencies only. That was likely a more significant stumbling block in my own life than I fully realized. There are entire books and courses on prayer, which can be helpful—or downright intimidating—but these written prayers were still scripts.

It didn't help that my religious experiences were with denominations that actively prayed preapproved prayers for specific situations. That kind of formality and legality is not required when praying to the Lord. Father God desires a personal relationship with all of His children. When we call upon His Name or invite Him to move on our behalf in a situation, I believe it proclaims His Lordship in our lives.

We can know God's heart and will for us. His ears are attentive to hear our hearts' cries, tears, and prayers. We can call on Him any time, day or night. I learned these essential concepts in 2016 as I practiced sitting quietly and expectantly at Jesus' feet in the 24/7-worship atmosphere at the International House of Prayer in Kansas City, Missouri.

As I sought the Lord, He started revealing hard truths about my actual condition. The Lord wanted my undivided attention. I needed wisdom and revelation, healing and breakthrough, which only come from learning to sit in the Lord's presence. It wasn't a time for running and doing—it was a time for resting and abiding. In that place, I learned nothing could compete with the magnificence of God's light and love.

As I learned to sit with God, I connected with the Lord's heart and fell in love with Him. I changed in His presence. Satan's deceptions and lies were exposed. The Lord led me in dealing with these deceptions. He didn't abandon me to figure things out on my own.

> The word of God, *you see,* is alive and moving; sharper than a double-edged sword; piercing the divide between soul and spirit, joints and marrow; able to judge the thoughts and will of the heart. No creature can hide from God: God sees all. Everyone and everything is exposed, opened for His inspection; and He's the One we will have to explain ourselves to. (Hebrews 4:12–13 VOICE)

As He walked with me and guided me through the steps of working out my salvation, I came to know Him as my Deliverer (Psalm 18:2). In book one of this series, I shared how the Lord liberated me from false belief systems to reveal Himself as my Healer (Exodus 15:26). The Lord is beautiful, and there are so many facets to God that we'll be learning new things about Him for all of eternity!

Jehovah Sit Canoe?

When Holy Spirit teaches me new things, He often has me repeat what He's saying. I love this process because it's one way I partner with God to exercise my spiritual senses! One fall afternoon in 2016, as I walked outdoors with the Lord, I heard Him say, *Jehovah Sit Canoe.*

At least that's what I thought He said. The Lord repeated the exact words many times, but that was the best I could do! I wondered, *What's Jehovah Sit Canoe?*

I did not know what God was saying, but He never got frustrated with me. When I got home, I wrote what I thought God was saying and asked Him for understanding in the matter. I later learned that He was revealing His name to me!

"Jehovah Sit Canoe" was *Jehovah Tsidkenu,* which means "THE LORD OUR RIGHTEOUSNESS" (Jeremiah 23:6 NKJV) or "GOD-Who-Puts-Everything-Right" (Jeremiah 23:6 MSG). The blood of Jesus makes us right with God. Our relationship with God is secure because of Christ's righteousness.

As the Lord continually reveals His nature and names to us, it broadens and strengthens our faith in Him. I believe the Lord was speaking to me through Psalm 7:9–10 to prepare me for a forthcoming season of testing. The righteousness of Christ tests the affections of our hearts and our level of trust in Him. It also tests the measure of love, mercy, and grace we extend to others.

Once and for all, bring to an end the evil tactics of the wicked! Establish the *cause* of the righteous, for you are the righteous God, *the soul searcher,* who tests every heart to examine the thoughts and motives. God, your wraparound presence is my shield. You bring victory to all who are pure in heart. (Psalm 7:9–10 TPT)

Growing in Prayer

Through relationships, we grow to know a person's true nature and character. The same is true in our relationship with God. When we have a limited view of who God is, we can unintentionally fall out of alignment with His will.

When I was a new Christian, I never considered asking God how He would have me pray through a particular situation. I've known many Christians who regularly pray for no trials, tests, persecutions, or hardships. They want to skip all the hard things, and they don't want their children or grandchildren to go through hard things either!

What does God's word say about this? If we never faced hardships, would we ever need to call on Jesus? God says we *will* have difficulties because they're essential for testing our faith (James 1:2–5). However, it doesn't mean that we have to go through the hard things alone.

> Yes, and all who desire to live godly in Christ Jesus will suffer persecution. (2 Timothy 3:12 NKJV)

> I have told you these things, so that in Me you may have [perfect] peace *and* confidence. In the world you have tribulation *and* trials *and* distress *and* frustration; but be of good cheer [take courage; be confident, certain, undaunted]! For I have overcome the world. [I have deprived it of power to harm you and have conquered it for you.] (John 16:33 AMPC)

Tests and trials allow us to exercise our spiritual senses and build up our faith muscles. If we genuinely believe that nothing is hidden from God, we can also trust that our trials do not take the Lord by surprise (Hebrews 4:13).

If we asked the Lord how He would have us pray, He might invite us to pray that we would pass the test the first time, so we don't have to repeat it. When Jesus comes back for His Bride, He's returning for a Bride who has made herself ready. He's coming back for a Bride who is fully mature, alive, committed to Him (Revelation 19:7), and in love with Him.

God has a purpose and a plan for using everything through which we've ever walked. He uses all of it to fulfill His purposes in the lives of those who love Him (Romans 8:28, Psalm 138:8). Contrary to how it often feels, life's tests are not meant to destroy us! God is not asking us to prove anything to Him—He already knows everything. So then, to whom do we need to prove ourselves? I believe that as we walk through tests and trials, God is revealing areas of potential growth to *us*. The tests are often for our benefit because they show or expose our beliefs, responses, and reactions.

The Benefits of Difficulties and Persecutions

In Matthew 26:39 (TPT), Jesus "prayed, 'My Father, if there is any way you can deliver me from this suffering, please take it from me. Yet what I want is not important, for I only desire to fulfill your plan for me.' Then an angel from heaven appeared to strengthen him." Jesus, the Son of God, knew He had a hotline straight to Heaven and that He could call on His Father. The same is true for all sons and daughters of God— we can call upon the Lord at any time.

What if, like Jesus, we only desired to fulfill the plans that God has for us? What if that was our ultimate faith goal?

Jesus is not unsympathetic to our circumstances and situations. He knows what it's like to emerge victorious after being tested. When Jesus prayed, an angel from heaven appeared to strengthen Him to fulfill God's will. I believe Jesus wants to help us have that same victory experience.

> For Jesus is not some high priest who has no sympathy for our weaknesses *and flaws*. He has already been tested in every way that we are tested; but He emerged victorious, without failing God. (Hebrews 4:15 VOICE)

When we fail, fall, face fear, or doubt—when we don't know what to do or who to call—we can always call on Jesus! God wants to be Lord over every area of our lives (Exodus 20:3, Zechariah 14:9, 1 Corinthians 8:6). Yes, by all means, call your best friend, the church prayer line, or anyone else who might stand with you in prayer for whatever you're going through, but before you do—call on Jesus.

What if our calling out to Jesus wasn't a cry for help but a confession of faith?

My friend, let's wise up to the enemy's tactics and stop being pushed around! It's God who restores us and strengthens us to fight the battles before us, but we are not fighting these battles alone. In Matthew 4, when the enemy tempted Jesus in the wilderness, Jesus countered every attack with, "It is written." We absolutely must have a personal relationship with Jesus, the Word, because we're fighting spiritual battles, not against flesh and blood.

> Take a decisive stand against him and resist his every attack with strong, vigorous faith. For you know that your believing brothers and sisters around the world are experiencing the same kinds of troubles you endure. And then, after your brief suffering, the God of all loving grace, who has called you to share in his eternal glory in Christ, will personally and powerfully restore you and make you stronger than ever. Yes, he will set you firmly in place and build you up. (1 Peter 5:9–10 TPT)

"Who Do You Say I Am?"

In Matthew 16:15 (paraphrased), Jesus asks His followers a question that I believe every Christian will one day have to answer, "Who do you say I am?" That's essentially the question that the Lord posed to me in 2015 when He asked, *Are you ever going to believe that I am who I say I AM?*

> When Jesus came to Caesarea Philippi, he asked his disciples this question: "What are the people saying about me, the Son of Man? Who do they believe I am?" They answered, "Some are convinced you are John the Baptizer, others say you are Elijah reincarnated, or Jeremiah, or one of the prophets." "But you—who do you say that I am?" Jesus asked. Simon Peter spoke up and said, "You are the Anointed One, the Son of the living God!" Jesus replied, "You are favored and privileged Simeon, son of Jonah! For you didn't discover this on your own, but my Father in heaven has supernaturally revealed it to you." (Matthew 16:13–17 TPT)

I opened this chapter by sharing a story of a confident young girl I met on a walking trail in 2018. She was secure in her father's love and authority. She knew he would take care of the issue with the overgrown path. How much more would our heavenly Father do for us if we called on Him (Matthew 7:11)? As we continue to grow in spiritual maturity, we are learning to trust God with *all* things. We are giving Him greater access to our hearts and aligning our will with His. We are learning to partner with—and receive from—the Lord.

Whatever measure of faith you have, I challenge you to be more intentional about spending time with Jesus. Ask Him how you should pray and invite Him to move in your situation. During your trials, ask God how He wants to reveal Himself to you. I believe the Lord reveals Himself to us to the degree that we seek Him.

What Does God Say About This Topic?

When the *righteous* cry for help, the Lord hears, *and* delivers them out of all their distress and troubles. (Psalm 34:17 AMPC)

Keep on asking and it will be given you; keep on seeking and you will find; keep on knocking [reverently] and [the door] will be opened to you. (Matthew 7:7 AMPC)

But everyone who calls on the name of the LORD will be saved. (Acts 2:21 NLT)

You shall call on me, and you shall go and pray to me, and I will listen to you. You shall seek me, and find me, when you search for me with all your heart. (Jeremiah 29:12–13 WEB)

Application Challenge

Read Romans 8:32. What does this reveal about your relationship with God? Is there anything that you can't take to Jesus? Are there any off-limits topics?

In Matthew 16:15 (paraphrased), Jesus asked his followers, "Who do you believe I am? Who do you say I am?" Ponder for a moment how you might respond to that question.

Journal and ask, "Lord, who do You want to be for me in this season of life?" "Jesus, what truth do you want me to know about You?"

What's your response time? How long is it after you first notice a problem before you call out to God? And how long are you willing to wait for Him to answer?

Let's Pray

Father God, we thank You for who You are. There is no other name like the Name of Jesus! You alone are all-powerful. You are brilliant! Lord, we confess that Jesus Christ is Lord over every area of our lives. We bind, now, in Jesus' Name, every mind-binding spirit that would attempt to come against us to prevent us from reading and understanding Your holy scriptures. Lord, we invite You to come close and make Your manifest presence known to us.

Thank You for allowing us direct and immediate access to Your heavenly hotline. Thank You that when we call, You always answer. You're never too busy to talk with us. You're concerned about everything that concerns us. We place our trust in You alone. We love You, and it's in the mighty Name of Jesus that we pray. Amen.

Chapter Four

There's Power in the Blood

The old church hymns reverberated with God's many Names, praising His nature, character, and all-sufficient power. When hymnals fell out of favor in churches all across America, we stopped singing "Power in the Blood."[3] Doing so left the next generations of Christians largely unaware of what *power in the blood* or *pleading the blood* means. It's an essential and effectual concept every Christian needs to understand because the power of the blood of Jesus is a valuable tool for fighting the enemy of our soul.

The information presented in this chapter builds upon the chapter on communion found in book two of this series. There, I reviewed what communion means, how it's connected with Passover, and what a blood covenant is.

Forgiveness of Sin—Redemption in Christ's Blood

God's forgiveness of our sins was part of Jesus' finished work on the cross. It's not based on anything that we have done or can do on our own—it's only possible because of the precious blood of Jesus.

> Since we are now joined to Christ,
> we have been given the treasures of
> redemption by his blood—the total
> cancellation of our sins—all because
> of the cascading riches of his grace.
> (Ephesians 1:7 TPT)

In Luke 15, the loving father shows compassion for his young son by running out to meet him. He embraces his son and covers him with his own robe (Luke 15:20–24 NKJV). Similarly, God embraces us in the compassion of His open arms of love, and it's the blood of Jesus that serves as our robe of righteousness (Isaiah 61:10 TPT). Nothing else will bring us eternal restoration. Jesus is the gate that we must go through (John 10:2–3), but it's God who leads us there.

We can trust the Lord will reveal who He is to us. It is Father God's delight to disclose truth to us, spend time with us, talk with us, and watch us grow in spiritual maturity. I believe Jesus wants us to be so close to Him that we not only know His heart, but we feel His heartbeat.

The Blood of Jesus Testifies of All the Promises of God

The blood of Jesus took care of all the issues—every single one—forever. Is there anything that the blood of Jesus has not already purchased or provided for us? He paid our sin debt in full. When the enemy tries to convince us we owe a debt or obligation of any kind, we need only take it to Jesus and release it to Him!

> How much more is done by the blood of Christ. He offered himself through the eternal Spirit as a perfect sacrifice to God. His blood will make our hearts clean from useless acts. We are made pure so that we may serve the living God. (Hebrews 9:14 ICB)

Jesus' blood redeems, purchases, and pays the price to free us from all sin debt that holds us enslaved by the enemy (Ephesians 1:7). The blood of Jesus frees us from our sins and speaks of forgiveness from Heaven. It justifies us and makes us right with Father God (Romans 5:9). The blood of Jesus washes us and makes us clean. This cleansing makes us holy, giving us confidence to approach God (Ephesians 2:13).

> And we have come to Jesus who established a new covenant with his blood sprinkled upon the mercy seat; blood that continues to speak from heaven, "forgiveness," a better

> message than Abel's blood that cries
> from the earth, "justice." (Hebrews
> 12:24 TPT)

For the first twenty years that I was a Christian, I don't believe I ever heard anyone say, "I plead the blood of Jesus over you." Primarily, I attended denominational churches where this phraseology wasn't typical. When I hear the word *plead*, it makes me think of a court case. Are you aware that God invites us to take matters to His Courts?

> For a day in Your courts is better
> than a thousand [anywhere else]; I
> would rather be a doorkeeper *and*
> stand at the threshold in the house of
> my God than to dwell [at ease] in the
> tents of wickedness. (Psalm 84:10
> AMPC)

I recall the first time Holy Spirit escorted me to the Courts of Heaven. Not familiar with the setting, I was totally and wholly dependent upon Him to guide me through the process. And why wouldn't He? Where He leads us, He's not setting us up to fail. In every case when the Righteous Judge has asked me to speak, I declare that Jesus, my Great Defender, will speak to the Courts on my behalf (Psalm 37:6, Hebrews 12:24). The Word of God ensures our victory.

Some Christians will use the phrase *plead the blood,* while others might say, "Appropriate the blood of Jesus." To *appropriate* something means to apply it. The Bride washes her own robes, but it's the blood that makes us spotless (Revelation 19:8, 22:14).

> *All that he does in us is designed* to make us a mature church for his pleasure, until we become a source of praise to him—glorious and radiant, beautiful and holy, without fault or flaw. (Ephesians 5:27 TPT)

When we say we are appropriating—or applying—the blood of Jesus over areas of our life, we're declaring that the price Christ paid was enough. The blood of Jesus forgives, delivers, heals, and protects to the uttermost and is the most powerful weapon we have against our enemy.

Several years ago, the Lord prompted me to pray for clarity of vision. It shifted more than my perspective. It also opened my eyes to see the enemy's deceptions. Increasingly, I'm learning that Satan only has the power we give him. The apostle Paul called our battle with Satan "hand-to-hand combat" (Ephesians 6:12 TPT). It often feels like that when the enemy trespasses. The real questions are, "What will we do when this happens? What will our reaction be? Will we stand and fight? Will we enforce his eviction?" Let me challenge you to think of spiritual warfare as enforcing property rights.

Property Rights and Property Management

Imagine that you own an extensive property. You've put out a sign that says NO TRESPASSING to let everyone know that the property is off-limits. However, people sometimes ignore signs and overstep boundaries. They may try to take things from the property that don't belong to them. In that case, you might call the police to evict the trespassing parties.

The matter may go to court. In a court setting, you'll be asked to provide proof of ownership and give your testimony. The judge will make a ruling based on the laws of the land and the evidence presented in court. The court's decree is binding and must be complied with.

Now, let's imagine a different scenario. You're taking care of a large estate for a wealthy property owner. This property owner has hired you to serve as estate manager—or overseer—and trusts you to care for his property as if it was your own.

In the first example, you wouldn't allow a trespasser to come onto your land to steal from you. You have authority over your privately owned property—your job description also grants you control over the estate property. Why, then, would you let a trespasser come onto the estate lands that you're responsible for managing?

You may wonder what this has to do with appropriating the blood of Jesus. Father God has granted His sons and daughters special authority as a benefit of the blood covenant. The blood of Jesus is available for all—and it covers every penalty of sin, including sickness and death (Psalm 107:19–

20). Still, we have an enemy who comes to steal, kill, and destroy (John 10:10). As born-again, Spirit-filled believers in Christ, we don't have to tolerate trespassers or squatters on anything entrusted to us.

The blood of Jesus covers all property—body, soul, spirit, health, wealth, well-being, finances, dwellings, and all of our belongings, every relationship, barns, storage buildings, livestock, and pets. The blood of Jesus covers every aspect of life when we become believers in Christ. When the devil trespasses in any area of a Christian's life, we have the authority to evict him. Sickness, disease, pain, premature death, accidents, and trauma are trespassers and must go at our command, in Jesus' name!

Jesus is the property owner—you are His estate manager!

> Now you understand that I have imparted to you all my authority to trample over his kingdom. You will trample upon every demon before you and overcome every power Satan possesses. Absolutely nothing will harm you as you walk in this authority. (Luke 10:19 TPT)

The spirit of death is a trespasser and must depart from every part of our lives. By pleading the blood of Jesus over our lives, we're letting Satan know his unfounded accusations must be withdrawn. Unless we open doors and allow him in, Satan has no right to rule the life of any blood-bought child of God.

Our job is to stay in perfect alignment and agreement with all that God says.

We can trust God with our life. He is the standard we follow, and we rest in His sovereignty. He is our plumb line (Zechariah 4:10 NKJV) and cornerstone (Ephesians 2:20 NKJV). As we work out our salvation, our mouths' confessions are increasingly being brought into alignment with the confessions of God's mouth. We're growing in wisdom, and understanding that we don't speak on our own. We speak as He speaks—and He speaks Heaven's language of love. Therefore, our testimony is always of the goodness and faithfulness of God. Our voices echo, amplify, and testify of Christ's Lordship.

The enemy will come to test our boundaries. Satan checks to see if we notice the trespass and how long we'll put up with it. When we appropriate the blood of Jesus, we're making a declaration. We're reminding the enemy that we know the truth of who we are in Christ, and we're enforcing our rights. We're saying, "This area is off-limits. The blood of Jesus covers it." Not only must the enemy leave, but if he caused any damage, he must make restitution. He must repay all that he has stolen *with interest* (Proverbs 6:31).

You may recall the story of Job. This would be an example of repayment with interest. God allowed Satan to test Job for some time. Even his friends *threw him under the bus!* But God restored Job completely when he released forgiveness and extended blessings upon those same "friends" who had spoken wrongly about him. After this, God restored to Job twice as much as before (Job 42:10).

How Does This Work?

If the concept of *pleading the blood* is new to you, you may wonder how this works. Just as we would do before partaking in communion, we want to ask God if any areas of our life are not aligned with His word or His ways. Is there any unconfessed sin in our life? Is there anyone we need to forgive?

If we're in right standing with God, then we can ask Him to direct our steps through appropriating (or applying) the blood of Jesus over our life. We ask God how He would have us pray. My friend, we can always call on Jesus and ask Him how He would have us respond to whatever situations we're facing!

When I ask God how He would have me pray, sometimes He has me plead or apply the blood of Jesus over every area of life. Sometimes Holy Spirit will say, *You know how to pray this,* or *You know what to do.* With God's guidance, I may plead the blood of Jesus from the crown of the head to the soles of the feet. Or I may declare or acknowledge that it's Jesus' blood that runs through my veins, DNA, and bone marrow.

Are we holding on to issues that don't belong to us? Are we withholding from Christ what belongs to Him—"issues" that He's paid to take from us and for us? Jesus' sacrifice at Calvary paid the price for us to be healed and set free from every form of bondage. When we apply the blood of Jesus, we're commanding the body to come into alignment with the perfect will of God. All sickness must go. Complete and total restoration must manifest at the cellular level; after all, it's Jesus' desire for us to be made "every whit" whole (John 13:10 KJV).

What is there that the blood of Christ hasn't provided, paid for, or covered? If there's an area of life where we're not walking in the abundant goodness of God (John 10:10), perhaps that's an area the Lord would have us apply the blood of Jesus. God knows His word. Satan and his minions know God's word. The real question is, "Do *we* know scripture?" And are we in a position to fight for what's rightfully ours? It's alright to remind God of His word in prayer but do so thoughtfully, filled with expectancy and faith to see it come to pass.

We want to have a good scriptural foundation for our prayers, particularly related to healing ministry and praying for others to be healed. When I first started praying for others to be healed, I felt a lot of pressure. That pressure wasn't from God. When I pray for others to be healed, I'm simply a vessel connecting people with God. It's a ministry of reconciliation (2 Corinthians 5:18–19). God is the only One with the power to heal, and power is in the blood of Jesus!

Provision is ours if we'll receive it. Believe and do not doubt in your heart that Heaven's provisions are for you, too. Let

God know you receive it by saying, "Thank You, Jesus."

What Does God Say About This Topic?

They conquered him completely through the blood of the Lamb and the powerful word of his testimony. *They triumphed because* they did not love and cling to their own lives, even when faced with death. (Revelation 12:11 TPT)

How much more is done by the blood of Christ. He offered himself through the eternal Spirit as a perfect sacrifice to God. His blood will make our hearts clean from useless acts. We are made pure so that we may serve the living God. (Hebrews 9:14 ICB)

He personally carried our sins in his body on the cross so that we can be dead to sin and live for what is right. By his wounds you are healed. (1 Peter 2:24 NLT)

He wore a robe dipped in blood, and his title is called the Word of God. (Revelation 19:13 TPT)

Application Challenge

If you're interested in learning more about the Courts of Heaven, you may appreciate Robert Henderson's resources on the topic.

Read Isaiah 53:4–5. Journal and ask, "Jesus, what did Your sacrifice of love accomplish for me?"

Journal and ask, "Lord, are there any trespassers I need to evict from the estate you have entrusted me to manage on Your behalf?"

Unforgiveness and lack of repentance give demonic spirits a legal right to enter your life. Journal and ask, "Lord, is there any unconfessed sin in my life? Is there anyone I need to forgive?"

Let's Pray

Father God, thank You for Your continual presence and Lordship. Your blood has redeemed us and delivered us from the hand of our enemy. We call on the blood of Jesus now to wage a continuous battle against Satan's evil schemes. Strengthen us, Lord, to resist the accuser's dark deceptions. We plead the blood of Jesus over all You have entrusted to us.

The blood of Jesus covers us completely, from the crown of our head to the soles of our feet. It protects our mind, will, and emotions, health, wealth, and relationships. We plead the blood of Jesus over all the generations of our bloodline. Negative and hostile forces, situations, or circumstances do not sway us. Lord, thank You for Your blood that has cleansed us from all sin and sealed us in Your covenant promises. It's in the all-powerful Name of Jesus we pray. Amen.

Chapter Five

Who Do You Think You Are?

God's view of us is often very different from our view of ourselves or others. In 2015, when God confronted my foundational beliefs, I didn't realize that a big part of my ongoing struggle was an orphan-spirit mindset. Mindsets are belief systems, and my wrong beliefs were considerable roadblocks that prevented me from living in God's fullness.

An orphan spirit would have us believe that God doesn't love us as we are. This faulty mindset can lead to striving or working towards earning salvation and sonship rather than accepting the finished work of Christ. An orphan spirit tells us we're unwanted and we don't belong.

The danger of holding on to wrong thoughts or beliefs is that they eventually become strongholds. Strongholds are not demons to be cast out; they're thought patterns rooted in lies and deceptions. These wrong mindsets, beliefs, and strongholds may have originated with us, or we may have inherited them from previous generations. Regardless of their origin, we need to deal with them to walk in the fullness of the believer's authority.

Strongholds are dismantled by the truth of God's word and broken when we receive His word as absolute truth. This is important. We must learn to think of ourselves in the same way God feels about us. We want our words to God, self, and others to overflow from a pure and healthy heart.

Have you ever asked God how He sees you? Not so long ago, when I asked the Lord this question, His answer challenged me. God's love toward us is everlasting (Jeremiah 31:3 NKJV). Father God loves us in the same way He loves Jesus. From the very beginning, the Lord created humankind in His image. Therefore, whatever we think or know about Him, we can think about ourselves (Genesis 1:26–27). The Lord wanted me to know that because I am one with Christ, "As He is, so am I."

> We are not like Jesus *was*, but because of grace, we are like he is *now*: pure and holy, seated in heaven, and glorified. (1 John 4:17 TPT, footnote)

If we believed that the Lord sees us just as He sees Jesus, would our lives change? Mine did. My first conviction was to clean up my mouth. If I wouldn't say it about God, I shouldn't say it about myself. If I wouldn't say it about Jesus, I shouldn't say it about His Body, the individual members of which Christ is the Head. As we intentionally seek God, He is faithful to reveal Himself to us. In the process of learning of

Him, we also learn about ourselves. It's a progressive revelation. It's impossible to go anywhere apart from God. Once that sinks in, you'll start noticing Him everywhere and in everything!

Can We See Our Reflection in God's Face?

On a recent Sunday morning, as I walked into the church, I noticed that the greeter at the door was wearing new glasses. His glasses were so clean they captured my attention! Not only could I see my reflection in the lenses, but I could also see everything in the background. The Lord used this encounter to speak to me prophetically.

God showed me that as we approach Him, we are looking into the mirror of who He is. In doing so, we can't help but see our reflection in His face. We discover who we are as we seek God's face because He created us in His image.

> We can all draw close to him with the veil removed from our faces. And with no veil we all become like mirrors who brightly reflect the glory of the Lord *Jesus*. We are being transfigured into his very image as we move from one brighter level of glory to another. And this

glorious transfiguration comes from
the Lord, who is the Spirit. (2
Corinthians 3:18 TPT)

The Word of God equips us and prepares us. When our lives
don't align with what God says in His Word, we can ask Him
to help us. God loves us so much that He will correct our
wrong ways of thinking. He will reveal any resistant or
rebellious areas that hinder us from walking in the fullness of
all He has for us.

What if someone gave you a puzzle, but they kept some of the pieces?

God revealed this truth to me one day through a puzzle
analogy. God sees the big picture and knows the end from the
beginning (Isaiah 46:10). He sees every part. While it may
seem like we're missing some pieces, God's word says
otherwise. Scripture tells us that God would withhold no good
thing from those who walk uprightly with Him (Psalm 84:11
paraphrased). What if someone gave you a puzzle, but they
kept some pieces? Who would do that? The Lord showed me
that this was how I was living my life. It's a question we must
ask ourselves—do we withhold some parts of the puzzle of
our lives from God?

In Christ, we already have access to all we will need for
living victoriously here on earth, just as we do in Heaven
(Luke 11:2). God wants to make us whole, but to do so, we
need to give Him all the pieces of our life.

> May God himself, the God who
> makes everything holy and whole,
> make you holy and whole, put you
> together—spirit, soul, and body—
> and keep you fit for the coming of
> our Master, Jesus Christ. The One
> who called you is completely
> dependable. If he said it, he'll do it!
> (1 Thessalonians 5:23–24 MSG)

Do we withhold access because we're afraid of what God will say? Do we fear His reaction or His rejection? God's love for us is unconditional. A few years ago, my beliefs were challenged in this area when I met a missionary evangelist visiting from overseas.

"At Least I'm Not a Murderer"

This young man was on fire for God, and he had a powerful testimony. He admitted that as a former Satanist, he committed certain horrific crimes. His family embraced the realm of darkness, and he had been groomed for an eventual leadership position in that arena. There were progressively greater dues, rituals, initiations, and investments required with each passing year.

An encounter with God changed him and caused him to fall off his high horse (Acts 9:3–9). Like the apostle Paul's

Damascus Road experience, this young man's change was instant and dramatic. It's easy to dismiss parts of the Bible written over two thousand years ago when you think it's describing a one-time event. Yet here was an instance when the presence of God showed up just as fiercely in modern times.

At that point in my life, many lies of the enemy replayed in a continuous loop in my head. I had listened to the accusations for so long that I believed I must be the biggest sinner in the entire world and that my sins were too great for redemption. Hearing the testimony of this young evangelist brought conviction. Though I've never physically murdered anyone, I was guilty of murdering others with my words.

> Death and life are in the power of the tongue, and they who indulge in it shall eat the fruit of it [for death or life]. (Proverbs 18:21 AMPC)

I first learned of the concept of *lashon ha'ra*, or evil speech, from a messianic Jewish teaching. This concept is familiar to believers of Jewish and Hebrew roots. When we speak words that are not aligned with God's truth, we risk dishonoring others and causing harm. This was the sin in my life that I thought was too great for God to forgive.

Well, at least I'm not a murderer was no longer a justification or excuse for holding on to sin or comparing sins with others.

Why do we even say things like that? The Lord forgave Saul for murdering Christians. He also gave Saul a new name—Paul—and powerfully used him to expand the Kingdom of Heaven on earth (Acts 9:21). I knew that Bible story, but I hadn't considered how it applied to life in the twenty-first century. God has not changed. What He did in "Bible times" He's still doing now.

This young man appreciated God's forgiveness of all his sins, and that was my conviction. *Did I have that same gratitude for all God had done in my life? Was I still listening to the lies of the enemy and living in bondage? Was I intentional about sharing my testimony with others? Was I on fire for God?*

I believed this young evangelist was telling the truth. God changed him. If God could forgive someone who had openly mocked Him, defiled His Name, and caused great harm to others, could I also believe that God would forgive me?

I sat with the Lord talking about these things. That day, God had access to parts of the inner depths of my heart I had kept blocked off and hidden from everyone for decades, and He led me to freedom.

> Grace has made former rebels into princes and princesses, royal ones that share in the inheritance of Christ. (Romans 8:17 TPT, footnote)

The young man's testimony revealed limitations I placed on God. Our God of hope restores to the uttermost all we dare to put in His hands (Romans 15:13 NKJV). Anything in our lives that we think is more prominent than God is a lie of the enemy. After all, what is there that's bigger than God? Satan is not God's equal. He's not even *our* equal (Romans 16:20).

Knowing our true identity as children of the living God (Hosea 1:10 NKJV) requires an investment in time spent with God and time in His word. It's a matter of intimacy (*into-me-see*) as we invite God to take possession of all He has purchased by granting Him access to all the puzzle pieces of our lives.

New Identity, New Destination

From day one of our salvation, we have a new identity in Christ. We have a unique role, a new position, a new name, and our eyes are fitted with new lenses to see as God sees. With a firm grasp of our new identity, the possibilities are endless!

When we don't know our identity as sons and daughters of God, we're not living up to our full potential. Christians under the influence of an orphan spirit are insecure in their character. They may be easily offended, prone to jealousy, anger, rivalry, have low self-esteem, have addictions, or struggle with unworthiness. The door to the orphan spirit ruling in a person's life may not have originated with that person. Previous generations may have also opened the door to an orphan spirit.

People who struggle under the influence of an orphan spirit may seek to find their identity in activities, roles, titles, appearances, or material possessions rather than God. Spirits of fear, rejection, failure, guilt, shame, unforgiveness, anger, jealousy, bitterness, judgment, insecurity, depression, and rebellion often accompany the orphan spirit.

As children of God, our identity is found in Christ alone. We're not trying to take our old views and ways into a new life with Christ. It's a lesson God has reinforced with me repeatedly. Deliverance often comes in layers. When our hearts and hands are full of "old," we're not in a position to grab hold of the "new" that God has for us.

> In the past you did not understand, so you did the evil things you wanted. But now you are children of God who obey. So do not live as you lived in the past. But be holy in all that you do, just as God is holy. God is the One who called you. It is written in the Scriptures: "You must be holy, because I am holy." (1 Peter 1:14–16 ICB)

The following middle-of-the-night confession I sent to myself, by talk-to-text message using my phone, clearly illustrates the internal struggle produced by these wrong mindsets.

Reflection and Correction, July 2018

Yesterday, I prayed in obedience on a couple of occasions. I delayed praying on one occasion. I'm sure I failed on several occasions as I stepped back because I didn't want to get in the way.

Is that how it's supposed to work? That's progress from last year, but I want to have a better record than that. God would do anything for me. Why won't I do anything for Him? I've got to get to the root of this fear. Fear is a liar, and I've got to let go of it. I want to let go of it and stop picking it back up. I want to walk on water.

Sometimes, God nudges me to do some things where I drag my feet. It's true. That's a big fat fail. I may get some things right, but there's probably double that amount behind the scenes that I talk myself out of. Am I the only one this happens to?

Partial obedience is disobedience. Partial truth is still a lie. Conditional love, which expects anything in return, is not accounted to us (Luke 6:34–35). It's not love at all. Why do I hesitate? Why do I question? Is it control, lack of trust, lack of faith, or "lack" in general? Downright unbelief? Fear? I don't know what it is!

The more time I spend with God, the more time I want to spend with Him, and it never seems like it's enough. Or, let's be honest here—there are some days that I stay busy doing many things but not accomplishing much because I'm avoiding God. There, I've said it. That's probably very comical to Him, as He has a habit of going everywhere with me and looking over my shoulder. The Lord whispers loving guidance in my ear—even when I refuse to sit with Him.

Still Growing

Do you ever review your life to see if you're making progress? Can you imagine that there was ever a time in my life when I didn't ask questions? It's true. I didn't ask questions, and I was stuck spinning my wheels in the muck. I don't want to be stuck or off track like that again. Not with God, so sometimes I ask, *Lord, are we good? Is everything okay between us? Lord, am I where I should be? Is this where I need to be right now?*

I don't want to carry around the garbage of my past. I want to move forward freely. I don't want to have open wounds that contaminate everyone and everything around me. I lived like that before, and it was messy. I don't want wrong beliefs or unbelief to impede all God has planned for me. Why do we struggle so much with believing in God? Why is it so challenging to trust in Him completely? That's the battle of the carnal mind and flesh (Romans 7:15–20 ICB). Self-centered focus only brings uncertainty, fear, disbelief, and questioning. When I turn my face *from* God, I lose sight of Him. When I'm looking to *me*, I'm tempted to retreat and run. There's only one way to recover.

It requires the "re-covering" of God's love and clothing myself in Christ's righteousness (Romans 13:14). When I miss the mark, I can change my mind and turn back to God. Father God's arms are always wide open to receive me (Luke 15:17–24).

God does not expect us to be perfect—we are being *perfected*. According to Hebrews 12:2 (NLT), it's Jesus who initiates and perfects our faith. God will teach us how to be free from our distractions so we can focus on Him. He will lead us to sit at His feet. He'll guide us through the processes of positioning ourselves to receive from Him. The Lord is faithful to teach us, but we're also learning from those who have gone before us (Hebrews 12:1–3). The Lord is rock solid and is not moved by our missteps or mistakes. God is serious about doing whatever it takes to guide us to the path of truth that allows us to fulfill our God-designed destiny and purpose.

But I come swiftly, so cling tightly to what you have, so that no one may seize your crown of victory. (Revelation 3:11 TPT)

When God says, "cling tightly to what you have," He's not referring to anything we might have in this world. He's referring to eternal truths. We cling to those things that are endless—these are the things that our enemy wants to steal, kill, and destroy. Satan and his minions attempt to distract us from our crown of victory and steal our confidence in God.

One of the easiest ways to lose what we've gained with God is for our words to betray God's Kingdom. Declarations reverberating with doubt, fear, and hate toward God or others make us traitors who have sided with His enemy. We put a stop to the influences of these lies when we take them to God.

Spirit of Adoption

We are not striving for God to like us better or to love us more. An orphan mindset tells us we have to excel at everything to earn God's love and attention.

In contrast, the spirit of adoption allows us to walk securely in the love and acceptance of Father God—which we're able to share with others freely! We trust God will guide our steps and that He has a plan to prosper us and protect us. The Lord is our Comforter, Counselor, and Friend. It is our joy to serve Him and co-labor with Him to serve others. With this mindset and attitude, we step into the rest of Christ.

> For those who are led by the Spirit of God are the children of God. The Spirit you received does not make you slaves, so that you live in fear again; rather, the Spirit you received brought about your adoption to sonship. And by him we cry, "*Abba, Father.*" (Romans 8:14–15 NIV)

When we resist and rebel against God, it dishonors Jesus' sacrifice and does not glorify God. It's the power of darkness at work in us that causes us to refuse to obey God, but the Lord has called us to follow Christ's example to overcome the world (John 16:33 NLT).

> For whatever is born of God overcomes the world. And this is the victory that has overcome the world —our faith. Who is he who overcomes the world, but he who believes that Jesus is the Son of God? (1 John 5:4–5 NKJV)

God has more for us, and He has best for us, though sometimes we are tempted to settle for good enough. We can trust that the Lord is always leading us forward on a beautiful, eternal journey of discovering our true identity in Him. In God's presence, there is no striving, no strings attached, nor fear of rejection. We are fully alive and wholly forgiven (Hebrews 1:1–4 NKJV). When we can receive these words as truth, it's like a heavenly chiropractic adjustment that brings us back into perfect alignment.

Positive Affirmations

As I began to break free from these wrong beliefs, the Lord led me to make daily declarations to affirm my true identity as His beloved daughter. Speaking these words aloud helped tremendously. Affirmations are declarations of truth, and they are useful reminders for helping us grow in our identity in Christ. While we're doing so, we're also memorizing scripture! When we sow the seeds of God's word in our hearts, there will be a day of great harvest! If you don't already make daily declarations or speak affirmations over your life, here are a few paraphrased scripture-based declarations you might consider.

I am a child of God. (John 1:12)

I am a member of Christ's body. (1 Corinthians 12:27)

I am complete in Christ. (Colossians 2:10)

I am free from condemnation. (Romans 8:1)

I am a citizen of Heaven. (Philippians 3:20)

I am born of God, and the evil one cannot touch me. (1 John 5:18)

I am God's temple. (1 Corinthians 3:16)

We are called to be Jesus' disciples—but orphan thinking will cause us to be His followers in name only. As we grow in confidence in God's love toward us, everything within us burns to share His transforming love with others. That is our co-mission with the Lord. Knowing our identity in Christ is an essential prerequisite for consistently walking in His authority and power, and it's the topic of our next chapter.

What Does God Say About This Topic?

For the Holy Spirit makes God's fatherhood real to us as he whispers into our innermost being, "You are God's beloved child!" And since we are his true children, we qualify to share all his treasures, for indeed, we are heirs of God himself. And since we are joined to Christ, we also inherit all that he is and all that he has. We will experience being co-glorified with him provided that we accept his sufferings as our own. (Romans 8:16–17 TPT)

So don't worry. For your Father cares deeply about even the smallest detail of your life. (Matthew 10:30–31 TPT)

But friends, that's exactly who we are: children of God. And that's only the beginning. Who knows how we'll end up! What we know is that when Christ is openly revealed, we'll see him—and in seeing him, become like him. (1 John 3:2 MSG)

But those who embraced him and took hold of his name he gave authority to become the children of God! (John 1:12 TPT)

And I will pray the Father, and He will give you another Helper, that He may abide with you forever—the Spirit of truth, whom the world cannot receive, because it neither sees Him nor knows Him; but you know Him, for He dwells with you and will be in you. I will not leave you orphans; I will come to you. (John 14:16–18 NKJV)

We also pray that you will be strengthened with all his glorious power so you will have all the endurance and patience you need. May you be filled with joy, always thanking the Father. He has enabled you to share in the inheritance that belongs to his people, who live in the light. For he has rescued us from the kingdom of darkness and transferred us into the Kingdom of his dear Son, who purchased our freedom and forgave our sins. (Colossians 1:11–14 NLT)

Application Challenge

Journal and ask, "Lord, what do you want to say about my identity and destination?" "Lord, I want You to have access to all the puzzle pieces of my life. Reveal to me any pieces I have hidden from You. Help me to see how You can use every part of my life for good."

Ask yourself these questions, "Am I focused on how big God is? Am I living from the place of God's provision and promises? Am I living overwhelmed by God or overwhelmed by the world? Am I living from the Father's presence as His daughter or son?"

As our revelation of the Spirit of Adoption (Romans 8:15) increases, we're able to share God's love more fully with others. What are some ways you might help a new believer in Christ learn about their Kingdom identity?

To learn more about the Jewish concepts of *lashon ha'ra* or *loshon hora* (evil tongue) and proper speech, you might refer to the classic *Chofetz Chaim: A Lesson A Day* by Rabbi Yisrael Meir Kagan (1873).

Let's Pray

Abba Father, there is none like You (Psalm 86:8). Your arms are wide open and ready to embrace us as we turn and "return" to You. Lord, we're sorry for the times we failed to recognize our true identity as Your beloved sons and daughters. Forgive us for the times we acted as though we were orphans. Thank You for pouring out Your Spirit of Adoption upon us (Romans 8:15 NKJV). The Light of Your presence dispels all darkness and guides us to victory. Lord, continue to expose any orphan thinking in our lives.

Breathe new-creation life into every part of Your Body. Grant supernatural increase of airflow and Holy Spirit movement in our lives to shift the atmosphere all around us. Thank You for the Spirit of Holiness who saturates our hearts and minds with the truth of who You are and who we are to You. Thank You for empowering us and giving us authority to devour the devourer to recover what is rightfully ours (Luke 10:17-19, Matthew 18:18, Malachi 3:11 NKJV, John 14:12).

Jehovah-Jireh, You are our daily provision. We are Your vessels. Mold us, shape us, and train us to carry Your glory in a way that honors You. When others encounter us, we want them to experience You. Lord, You have loved us so much that You gave all that was dear to You (John 3:16). Teach us to do the same (Mark 14:6). Lord, we praise You. It's in the mighty Name of Jesus we pray. Amen.

Chapter Six

Walking in Authority and Power

The communion service at church had just ended. I lingered in the Lord's presence near the altar. On that September evening in 2020, a heavenly portal opened. I watched with awe and expectancy as an angel stepped toward me. He held gifts in his arms, and he was extending them to me.

The first gift he presented was a heavenly scroll. I unrolled the legal-paper-sized scroll and discovered an arrest warrant. GALAXY-WIDE JURISDICTION, it stated. This arrest warrant granted "full authority to disarm, silence, and apprehend the enemy." The next item the angel handed me was a race baton. Last, he presented me with a signet ring. The angel communicated to my spirit that Jesus was inviting me to engage with Him. I placed the ring on my finger. It was a perfect fit! *Wearing this ring would identify me as Christ's ambassador*, the angel said. These gifts were tools to equip me for the tasks set before me in the days ahead. I nodded my head to show I had received the gifts. I didn't think to ask the angel for additional instructions.

I lingered in that place until the church doors closed, then I continued my conversation with the Lord at home. Gifts from God are unique invitations to commune with the Giver. I didn't want to assume that I knew or understood why God gave them or how He intended me to use these gifts. Only the Giver can provide the clarity, instruction, and wisdom for the provision's purpose.

We know that the Word of God is alive and active (Hebrews 4:12 NIV). God will use our sanctified imagination to reveal greater insight and understanding. God has already fully provided for all our needs, and we can carry out every mission and assignment successfully as we step into God's provision by faith.

I know what an arrest warrant is (Colossians 2:14 TPT), but I was unsure of other words written upon the scroll. According to Merriam-Webster's online dictionary, *apprehend* means to seize, either physically or mentally; to arrest; to perceive; to become aware of; to grasp with understanding, or to recognize the meaning of.[4]

Batons go to those running the race, not spectators (Hebrews 12:1, 2 Timothy 4:7, Philippians 3:14). I understood I had to do my part, but my part was just a tiny portion of a much bigger race. The baton was also a reminder that I'm not running the race alone. I'm part of a team, and that team is counting on me to be prepared and focused.

A signet ring is often used as a seal and represents governmental authority (Esther 8:8 NKJV).

How did these three gifts apply to scripture? As I sat with God and my Bible, I paid careful attention to the Lord's directions. This process requires listening for what the Lord is saying, then seeking confirmation from His written word. For some people, this means that the scriptures seem to *leap off the page*. For me, the scriptures might be highlighted yellow or feel weightier than the other texts around them. When this happens, it's like we're experiencing these scriptures from Heaven's perspective.

A few years ago, as the Lord spoke to me about His Great Commission, He did so by saying "co-mission." When He directed me as His ambassador to represent Him to others, He called me to "re-present" Him. It brought great clarity to see and hear His words in this way.

In Matthew 28:18–20, Jesus commissioned all who believe in Him to go in His authority. Although signet ring, arrest warrant, and baton are not explicitly mentioned in this text, I could see how it might apply with carrying out Christ's co-mission.

> Then Jesus came close to them and said, "All the authority of the universe has been given to me. Now wherever you go, make disciples of all nations, baptizing them in the name of the Father, the Son, and the Holy Spirit. And teach them to

YOU CAN SHARE THE LOVE OF GOD WITH OTHERS

faithfully follow all that I have commanded you. And never forget that I am with you every day, even to the completion of this age." (Matthew 28:18–20 TPT)

Christians are soldiers in the Lord's army (1 Peter 4:1 TPT). It's our duty and honor to guard all God entrusts to us. In our faithful service to Him, we find that all of life is ministry, and everywhere our feet tread is our mission field. We're stewards who take risks and multiply. The Captain of our salvation (Hebrews 2:10 NKJV) sends us out into all the world on a mission to share the good news with everyone. Are you ready to run?

Does walking in authority and power (Matthew 16:15–19) seem overwhelming? The disciples walked with Jesus and watched firsthand as He performed miracles. They grew to believe that this was normal for Jesus. Later, Jesus stretched their beliefs when He challenged them to do the same. They stepped out to try the impossible under His watchful supervision. But then, Jesus empowered them to go on their own. He kept encouraging them to grow! He does the same for us, too!

So you see, faith by itself isn't enough. Unless it produces good deeds, it is dead and useless. Now someone may argue, "Some people have faith; others have good deeds." But I say, "How can you show me your faith if you don't have good deeds? I will show you my faith by my good deeds." (James 2:17–18 NLT)

Faith requires a response. It calls for stepping out and taking risks. When we unpack the gifts of God, Holy Spirit batteries are included, powered up, and ready to go. The invitation is to join Him. Like a baby who holds tight to Daddy's fingers as she's learning to take her first steps, we can trust that God is with us as we grow. What has all this got to do with walking in spiritual authority and power? More than we often realize.

Dare to Believe God for More

If supernatural signs accompany whoever believes, and God's word is accurate, then something wasn't adding up. In 2014, when my mother was in immeasurable pain and dying of cancer, I felt helpless. She had been unable to speak in the days leading up to her death. My prayers were twofold, and God answered both in a magnificent way. I wanted my Mom to feel and know the manifest presence and love of God. I also asked the Lord to assure me of her salvation.

On the day my Mom died, God's love and glory so wholly and powerfully manifested within, on, and around her that words cannot describe what took place. It was weighty and glorious. My mother passed from this life to the next with a smile on her face. Truly, she never looked more beautiful or at peace.

> *But in the depths of my heart I truly know* that you, Yahweh, have become my Shield; You take me and surround me with yourself. Your glory covers me continually. You lift high my head. I have cried out to you, Yahweh, from your holy presence. You send me a Father's help. *Pause in his presence.* (Psalm 3:3–4 TPT)

Praying for a creative miracle (Luke 13:12 TPT) or resurrection life (Luke 7:12-15) never crossed my mind. Even though I attended church faithfully, my regular seat was on the proverbial fence of indecision. Wasn't praying for healing like playing the lottery—a one-in-a-million chance of winning for anyone without a hotline straight to heaven? Holding tight to a frustrating and powerless form of Christianity, I continued drifting in the enemy's oceans of deception.

When God confronted me a year later in 2015, He was fully aware of my many false beliefs. Still, He threw me a lifeline when He challenged me to believe that He is who He says He is. Saying *yes* to Him changed my life. In the five short years since that reviving confrontation, God has never changed—but boy, I sure have! My faith continues to grow as I sit with my Bible and allow the Lord to establish my feet upon His firm foundation.

By faith, we receive, are healed, and prosper. We cannot reason or comprehend all that God is or how He will do what He said He would do in our present state. It's not for us to figure out—we only trust and believe that He will do it—and we keep our eyes fixed on Jesus.

We base our ministry upon the finished works of Christ (John 19:30 NKJV). He has already triumphed over every power of darkness (Colossians 2:15 TPT). New life flows from the Holy Spirit within us and empowers us to be transformed into greater levels of glory. Not only do we have the perceptions and mind of Christ, but we see as God sees. We are clothed in His righteousness and impart His fragrant aroma everywhere we go (2 Corinthians 2:15–16 TPT).

> But God chose those whom the world considers foolish to shame those who think they are wise, and God chose the puny and powerless to shame the high and mighty. (1 Corinthians 1:27 TPT)

Jesus encourages us to discern who we're following and on what we're focused. We are not following men, but God may use men to draw us nearer to Him. I want to stand with the faith-filled great cloud of witnesses whose lives are like directional arrows pointing the way to Jesus (Hebrews 12:1).

Basic First Aid for Christians

I love how The Passion Translation Bible refers to God as "my first responder" (Psalm 22:24). He is the One we must go to first in all things. Have you ever considered that while ministering to others in prayer, we're conducting a kind of first aid for healing?

"Hey, are you okay?"

One of the initial concepts taught in a first aid class is how to approach a person who appears to be injured. We might tap the person gently on the shoulder, make eye contact, and ask, "Hey, are you okay?" We're also encouraged to scan the surrounding area to see what else might be happening. We're looking for clues in the environment. There's an awareness and intentionality involved.

We may similarly deal with spirit-realm issues. As we approach a person, we're already having a silent conversation with the Lord about how He sees the person or situation and how He would have us respond. Holy Spirit reveals insights, wisdom, and understanding to us. The Lord activates our spiritual senses so that we're aware of what we're facing.

Do we have to reveal everything we might sense to the person to whom we're ministering? Not unless God directs us to do so. At all times, we remain in prayerful conversation with God, actively listening for His guidance and direction. The Lord often shows me a picture of what He would have me do, or He may give me the words to speak (John 5:19, 6:38,12:49). He'll do the same for you, too.

As a born-again Christian, I'm learning to keep my eyes focused on the light of God. Ultimately, my words and actions must be an accurate reflection of the One I represent.

> But all things are from God, Who through *Jesus* Christ reconciled us to Himself [received us into favor, brought us into harmony with Himself] and gave to us the ministry of reconciliation [that by word and deed we might aim to bring others into harmony with Him]. (2 Corinthians 5:18 AMPC)

Several years ago, in a church meeting, the pastor's wife shared this helpful direction. When sharing things we observe with our spiritual senses, we must learn to ask before speaking. *Is what I'm about to say true?* If not, stop right there. If yes, ask yourself, *Is it helpful?* While it may be true, it might not be beneficial. If it's not helpful or something we would expect to hear Jesus say, then stop right there. If it's accurate and useful, then ask yourself, *Is it my place to say it?* This last question is critical to ask when we're tempted to share something God has revealed.

When God speaks to us and allows us to see or hear what's going on with another person, He doesn't always mean for us to share it. We can't assume that's the case. However, God always invites us to pray about it and respond in a way that glorifies His Name.

God never intends for a shared insight to become a matter of gossip, to be used to judge someone negatively, or to cause a person to stumble or be alienated from Him (1 Timothy 5:13 TPT). We must be mindful as we're ministering to others to do so in a way that preserves their dignity, restores their honor, and adds no harm.

People or Projects? Time for a Heart Check!

My prayer life suffered from developmental delays for many years, primarily due to lack of use. I wasn't exercising my faith muscles or opening my mouth to speak to God. Regrettably, not all American churches use prayer teams or offer new Christians opportunities to partner with more mature Christians to learn how to pray. It's pretty unfortunate because there is great value in having an active prayer life.

My experiences with receiving prayer—when available— have also been varied. There's a noticeable difference when someone offers to pray because their heart is full of compassion or offering with hidden motives—like media recognition or pride.

The Lord's corrections brought valuable insight several years ago when I served as an event photographer at a women's retreat. The event was being documented and recorded for media promotion. I had already photographed the venue, as well as the attendees engaged in various activities.

During a time of early afternoon worship, Holy Spirit's presence grew heavy as the group prayed from their seats. Prayers went up, and tears flowed down in beautiful adoration of our God and King. The moment I lifted my camera to take photos, there was a check in my spirit.

A *check* is like a heavenly traffic light that has shifted from green to yellow and may turn red at any moment. It's an internal signal to slow down—a warning that something is about to come to a screeching halt. On this day, it was the Lord preserving the preciousness of what He was doing at that moment.

God directed me to set my camera aside and invited me to join in. He blocked me from being an unnecessary distraction. He showed me clearly that He valued and honored the souls of His beloved children more than media photos. It was a powerful lesson from God that His children are not projects, numbers, or dollars—they deserve to be treated so much better.

What if we treated everyone we encounter as if we were talking to or interacting with Jesus Himself (Matthew 25:40)?

We don't want to be people who only interact with others when the cameras are filming. We want to show others the authentic love of Christ (Philippians 2:3–5 TPT).

When we think of being good stewards of all God has entrusted to us, we often only think of material possessions or finances. Still, the people and relationships God has placed in our lives are our most significant responsibility. It's also a great honor.

It's not about the spotlight or fame. Everything we say and do should point others back to God. It's always only about God. What if we stopped living like we were self-employed but worked with the Kingdom of God in all things? What if we actively partnered with God to build, preserve, and expand a Kingdom culture of faith here on earth? Have we lost sight of our Great Commission?

> Examine your motives to make sure you're not showing off when you do your good deeds, only to be admired by others; otherwise, you will lose the reward of your heavenly Father. (Matthew 6:1 TPT)

> And I have come out of heaven not
> for my own desires, but for the
> satisfaction of my Father who sent
> me. (John 6:38 TPT)

Firm Faith Foundations

The unstable foundations of my faith left me on shaky ground for decades. When we know our identity in Christ, we understand our authority as believers. This shift in perspective is fundamental if we genuinely desire to grow in spiritual maturity.

Many Christians feel ill-equipped for spiritual warfare, but what if we considered it a matter of enforcing our spiritual authority instead? Jesus has already won the battle (John 16:33) and granted us authority to use His Name when we pray. Essentially, Jesus has granted us a divine power of attorney! The Lord has given us authority (or dominion) over all the power of the enemy to speak and carry out His business here on earth. God has entrusted us to enforce the victory He's already won, and we do so with our words.

> When the seventy disciples returned,
> they joyfully reported to him, "Even
> the demons obey us when we use
> your name." "Yes," he told them, "I

saw Satan falling from heaven as a flash of lightning! And I have given you authority over all the power of the Enemy, and to walk among serpents and scorpions and to crush them. Nothing shall injure you! However, the important thing is not that demons obey you, but that your names are registered as citizens of heaven." (Luke 10:17–20 TLB)

Jesus was fully aware of all that was going on in the spiritual realm, yet He focused on His Father. Did Jesus go around telling everyone that He was leading a healing and deliverance ministry? No! Instead, Jesus ministered love through prayer, and it was God's love that brought healing, deliverance, reconciliation, and restoration. Had I been standing in a dark room for so long that I failed to see this?

In 2018, when the Lord directed me to *focus on the light*, it sounded simple enough, but it challenged me. What did He mean—and how would this look? Seeing what's in the dark can be helpful for fighting what's in the dark, but it also has a way of pushing us toward being overly sin-conscious. When our focus is on darkness, everything becomes a sin issue, and our prayers become all about fighting the demonic. Instead of bumping into things in the dark negativity around us, wouldn't it be so much easier to flip on the *Light switch?* It's a concept I'm still learning.

The eye is the lamp of the body. *You draw light into your body through your eyes, and light shines out to the world through your eyes.* So if your eye is well *and shows you what is true,* then your whole body will be filled with light. (Matthew 6:22 VOICE)

My journey of learning about spiritual authority and warfare started at a small nondenominational church that addressed the demonic straight on. When God directed me to leave that church, the place He led me to next focused on facilitating healing very differently.

Pastors at that next church prayed for healing by declaring scriptures over a person. Disease is an abnormal or harmful condition that prevents the body from functioning properly. A few years ago, the Lord showed me that word as "dis-ease." *Dis-ease* is an uneasy feeling attached to anything that makes life more difficult. At this church, darkness and dis-ease often weren't addressed. This method certainly seemed more conducive to preserving a person's dignity and honor. It gave me something new to consider. The following testimony highlights this concept perfectly.

Testimony of Growth, July 2020

As I traveled along an unfamiliar stretch of highway in Arkansas, I felt a sudden and distinct shift in the atmosphere. It was as if I had crossed an invisible territorial line. Peace was pushed aside as I suddenly encountered spirits of heaviness and depression.

The Lord's wisdom shined down on me at that moment! Instead of addressing those negatives directly, I simply spoke aloud, "Spirit of gladness rest over this place. Spirit of gladness hover over this place and produce something new."

I don't recall *ever* praying that way before! Not only was it easy, but it also produced a powerful, immediate, and undeniable shift in the atmosphere!

What was God teaching me in that instance? Even though I may be aware of the presence of darkness, I can fight it by calling in replacements. I had taken this same test many times already, and this was my highest score yet!

I call for enforcements and "re-enforcements" of what God has already spoken. When I sense a spirit of darkness, I'm learning it's an invitation to shine the light of God in that place or over that situation. Essentially, I'm declaring the opposite of the thing I'm sensing. My job is to remain focused on the eternal and unstoppable Light and love of Christ.

> The Light shines on in the darkness,
> and the darkness did not understand
> it *or* overpower it *or* appropriate it *or*

absorb it [and is unreceptive to it].
(John 1:5 AMP)

Testimony of Healing from Inflammation, 2019

Right in the middle of folding laundry, I heard in my Spirit, *What's eating you?*

Not everything that I see, hear, or feel in the spirit realm is for me. It may be for someone else's benefit, but I may not know it until I ask God for clarity. I wrote these words in my journal and invited God to grant insight into what He would have me to do with this word.

My answer came the very next day as I stopped to talk with a family in the neighborhood. I hadn't planned on stopping, but it was a lovely day, and I saw them sitting on the porch. When I stopped to say "Hi," I didn't realize it was a God appointment.

As we casually chatted about a nearby construction project, I couldn't help but notice that the man was nervously scratching his arms. Quite unexpectedly, the Lord opened my spiritual eyes to see foamy-looking worms crawling out of his skin.

The Lord whispered, *Inflammation.*

I tried to ignore it, but it wouldn't go away. I have a face that speaks on its own. I could sense my expression changing in reaction to what I was seeing. Interrupting our conversation, I asked, "Can I pray with you?"

The man said, "Yes, sure," and he let me know he believed in Jesus. These spirit worms started manifesting even more, and they were flat-out gross!

Quietly on the inside, I talked with God about it, and I waited for the Lord's instructions. That's when He showed me what to do. I could see myself reaching over to brush the worms off the man's arms. These kinds of brief visions or pictures are battle strategies. The Lord's shared insights give us victory.

I asked the man for permission to touch his arms. His wife sat in the chair beside him, watching intently. I reached out to place my hands on the man's arms and gently began scooping up and brushing away things that no one else could see. It was all amazingly awkward and incredibly unpleasant!

When I did and said all that the Lord guided me to do, I asked the man if he felt any change. His response surprised me. He said he felt a lot of heat and a strong sense of peace. He said his arms had itched for about eight years for no apparent reason, but just as I prayed, all the itching had stopped. We marveled at what the Lord did and said, "Thank You, Jesus!"

I didn't stick around much longer. God gave this couple something to consider, and He showed His love for them through me.

I want people to be made well, but I also don't want to freak them out too much by doing peculiar things. Although biblical, I don't want to spit on the ground to make mud for their eyes (John 9:6); stick my fingers in their ears, or spit and then touch their tongue (Mark 7:33). God will often ask us to do or say things that can be uncomfortable. In this situation, God simply asked me to wipe away some invisible worms.

Once home, I pondered what the Lord was teaching. Stress can cause inflammation, and often results from holding on to unresolved issues. The effects of stress manifest differently in all of us. This man had sores that looked like cigarette burns on his arms. He said they itched all the time, so he scratched them. It was an autoimmune disorder that resulted in a type of psoriasis.

When prescriptions and traditional treatments fail to help, there's a good possibility there's a spiritual root manifesting physical symptoms. Autoimmune disease is essentially the body rejecting the body. The body is responding to the mind's thoughts. When we struggle with our identity, there is often self-hatred or rejection, which often leads to fear or anxiety regarding how others perceive us.

> There is no fear in love; but perfect love casts out fear, because fear has punishment. He who fears is not made perfect in love. (1 John 4:18 WEB)

This neighbor had been experiencing some sort of stress-induced irritation that wasn't properly or adequately dealt with, resulting in inflammation. After some time, the inflammation manifested itself physically as sores, which spiritually appeared as foamy, worm-looking creatures. I didn't know this man's history, nor did the Lord reveal it to me.

The Lord often answers prayers by sending people to our aid. Not everyone is open to receiving from the Lord, but this man was. Healing miracles like this demonstrate the reality of God's Kingdom and the great love our Father God has for all His beloved children.

Testimony of Healing at a Doctor's Appointment, 2018

I don't think God minds us getting medical help from doctors. We go to God first in all things, but God can, and does, use doctors to bring healing, as well.

I went in for a routine annual exam. The same technician had been on staff at that location for several years. There was always a calendar of nature scenes with scriptures hanging on her office wall, and I had long suspected she was a Christian. Before leaving her office that day, I felt the Lord nudging me to ask if she needed prayer for anything. I had never felt led to pray with her before.

The technician responded positively and asked if I might pray for God's blessings in her life. That's when Holy Spirit impressed upon me to ask if she needed physical healing in her body.

"Actually," she said, "I need knee replacement surgery—I've kept putting it off." She explained the issue was more than ongoing physical pain. It was that she needed *both* knees replaced, and she wasn't sure if her insurance would cover the cost of the procedure. Not only that, she wasn't sure she could afford the insurance co-pay. She wondered if there would be a penalty for missing so many workdays—would her employer hold the job for her? Or would they hire someone else while she was out?

Well, this was a lot bigger than "pray for the Lord's blessings to be upon my life!" Even while the technician was still sharing the details, I already heard God speak. With clarity, He said, *It is finished* (John 19:30).

All hesitation evaporates when the Lord speaks! As I placed my hands on her knees and prayed for God to make them new, I felt Him answer the prayer immediately. I felt those hot, swollen knees become lubricated with a honey-thick anointing from heaven!

I asked the technician what she was feeling. She stood with her eyes closed as I prayed. She said the pain had left, and she could feel something dripping down her knees. Yes, that's what I was feeling, too!

Was it a long prayer? No, I'm sure it wasn't, but this beautiful daughter of God was healed and made whole. In an instant, God's love had canceled out all worries. She had new knees, and it had taken less than a minute from start to finish. Her savings account and job were safe. She believed and received, according to her faith (Luke 13:12, Mark 5:34).

I had encountered this same technician half a dozen times over the years, and this was the very first time God ever prompted me to ask if I could pray for her. It left both of us praising the Lord!

In Conclusion

Walking in our spiritual authority as believers in Christ is powerful and exciting! It's part of God's Great Commission to all believers (Mark 16:15–18). Expanding the Kingdom of God is something that happens within us, but it's also about pointing others to Christ. It's about continually enlarging and inhabiting the territory God has established for us and multiplying or growing all He has entrusted us to steward on His behalf.

Even in reviewing journal notes to share in this chapter, I see my faith has grown tremendously in just a short amount of time. I encourage you to keep a written record of your faith journey and then review the pages periodically to see how far you've come. It's a beautiful, exhilarating adventure with God!

What Does God Say About This Topic?

You have chosen us to serve our God and formed us into a kingdom of priests who reign on the earth. (Revelation 5:10 TPT)

And the second command is like the first: "Love your neighbor as you love yourself." (Matthew 22:39 ICB)

For he has not despised my cries of deep despair. He's my first responder to my sufferings, and when I was in pain, he was there all the time and heard the cries of the afflicted. (Psalm 22:24 TPT)

That evening the people brought to him many who were demonized. And by Jesus only speaking a word of healing over them, they were totally set free from their torment, and everyone who was sick received their healing! (Matthew 8:16 TPT)

I admit that I haven't yet acquired the absolute fullness that I'm pursuing, but I run with passion *into his abundance* so that I may reach the purpose for which Christ Jesus laid hold of me to make me his own. I don't depend on my own strength to accomplish this; however I do have one compelling focus: I forget all of the past as I fasten my heart to the future instead. (Philippians 3:12–13 TPT)

Application Challenge

Journal and ask, "Lord, I want to be fully prepared for missions and ministry. Is there something that You would like me to start (or stop) doing to get ready for these important assignments? How can I grow with You? Are there any details of the last assignment I've left unfinished? What is the next adventure You have for me?"

What does *believing God* mean to you?

Do you have a testimony of healing to share with others? If you were talking with a pre-Christian (someone who doesn't know God yet), what's one thing you would share with them about your experience with God?

Are there any identifiable areas of darkness in your life right now? What would be the opposite of this? Ask the Lord how He would have you pray. How is He directing you to shine His Light in that place?

Let's Pray

Father God, we thank You for grace to walk in the fullness of Your love and power. Lord, forgive us for the times when we misrepresented You to others. Thank You for Holy boldness and courage to step forward in all You have predestined for us.

Strengthen us to rise and stand firm as we fasten our faith to You alone. May our words and actions honor, encourage and aid others to be restored to You. Fill our hearts and hands with hope and love, Abba, for Your glory. It's in the all-powerful, all-sufficient Name of Jesus we pray. Amen.

Chapter Seven

Obedience and the Great Commission

Many people ask if getting started in the ministry of healing was easy for me to do. Absolutely not, but not because God made it hard. I made it hard. I had many wrong belief systems that required overturning.

> The weapons of the war we're fighting are not of this world but are powered by God and effective at tearing down the strongholds *erected against His truth.* We are demolishing arguments and ideas, every high-and-mighty philosophy that pits itself against the knowledge of *the one true* God. We are taking prisoners of every thought, *every*

emotion, and subduing them into obedience to the Anointed One. (2 Corinthians 10:4–5 VOICE)

I'm grateful for having access to journal entries reflecting my thought processes along the way. Even though there were many times I hesitated, doubted, and questioned what I believed, there was steady forward-moving progress. Reviewing old journal entries provided insight into hidden negative patterns—and I knew to take those matters straight to God to exchange false views for the truth of His word.

I encourage everyone to document their dreams, visions, testimonies, and prophetic words as quickly as possible after they occur. This helps to preserve every precious detail of our encounters and interactions with God. Years later, as we review our notes, it imparts such a sweet blessing.

The first time I ever prayed with anyone in public was not something I left home thinking about doing. I needed to wash quilts before storing them away for the summer. They were too large for my washer and dryer at home, so I packed up my things and stopped by a local laundromat to use their oversized washers. I typed the testimony notes on my computer that evening as I reflected on the day's events.

Testimony of Healing, April 2017

I opened the door to the laundromat and stepped inside. A woman hurriedly approached me and said, "I was waiting for you." I had never seen this woman before, but I smiled and said, "Hi."

The woman came closer and repeated her statement. "I was waiting for you." Only this time, she added, "Can you help me?" We were the only two people in the building.

It was apparent that English was not her primary language. She explained she needed help loading and starting the washers. Not that she didn't know how to work the machines —the problem was that she could not raise her arms high enough to do it herself. I agreed to help.

As I was dropping quarters into the machines, I felt Holy Spirit nudging me to pray with her. I resisted. *What will I say? I don't even know what to say. I don't know her. What if she says no?* I tried hard to talk myself out of it, and I offered many lame excuses. I was still having this internal conversation with the Lord as I made my way over to the waiting area.

Taking a seat, I stared blankly out the window. My thinking soon shifted from *What if God doesn't heal her?* to *What if God does? What if God did what His word says He will do? What if I believed Him for it?* It was only a few days since I attended the "How to Heal the Sick" conference, where I saw people get healed. Here was an opportunity to pray with someone for healing!

What if God did what His word says He will do, and I believed Him for it?

That was me coming to my senses! I approached the woman to ask if I could pray for her. She nodded and told me her name was Lupe. Unsure of what to say next, I prayed in my prayer language.

I felt like I had fumbled my way through it and turned my attention back to laundry. I removed my quilts from the washers and transferred them into nearby dryers. My new friend would need help moving her laundry from the washing machines, too. I walked over to gather up her things. She followed me to the clothes dryers and said she thought she could manage it by herself.

Walking back to the waiting area, I sat down and was soon distracted by my phone. A few minutes later, I looked up and was surprised to see Lupe at the other end of the building, laughing and clapping her hands. She was waving her arms over her head.

Was she trying to get my attention? I didn't know if she needed help or not, so I got up from my seat and walked toward her. That's when it hit me—God had healed her! When I first met her, she was unable to lift her arms above her shoulders. Now, she was celebrating by dancing and singing, "Thank You, Jesus!"

She looked straight at me. Her eyes were as wide as saucers —and she asked if I would pray for her knees, too. "Yes, of course!" We walked to the nearest chairs, where she sat as I prayed for her knees. Immediately, Lupe jumped up and started doing knee bends to test it. That's some kind of faith for a woman who must have been at least seventy years old!

The first person God had me pray with outside of a church setting was a precious older woman who spoke Spanish. English was her second language, but she got very talkative after God healed her. Lupe went into a lot of detail about her medical history, pausing periodically to praise God. She said she could hardly believe God healed her *there* in the laundromat! She said she couldn't wait to go home to tell everyone what had happened.

It didn't matter that I prayed in tongues. I could hardly understand her, and she could barely understand me. There was no need to worry if I had done it wrong. It was less about me and more about God. The Lord will meet us in the place of our little faith and cause it to grow. Praying with a stranger was uncomfortable, but it wasn't difficult. I'll keep trying!

Testimony of Healing, January 2019

I typed out the details of this testimony on my computer about two hours after it took place.

I went out today to get a few groceries. The last item on my list was dog treats. Four stores later, no dog treats! I finally ended up at a store near home. By then, it was midafternoon. I thought, *I should have just gone home,* but then—something shifted as I stood in the checkout lane that made me think I wasn't there for the dog treats. It was a God appointment.

The lane next to me was closed, but a woman was standing in that space, holding a young boy. This child was having a breakdown—or was it a meltdown? A tantrum? I wasn't sure. Whatever it was, he was screaming at the top of his lungs with his arms and legs flailing as he resisted being held. The woman was trying hard to hold on to the boy and calm him down. People were watching. *Lots* of people were watching, stopping, and gawking. The cashier asked me if someone should try to help. *Why was she asking me?* I thought the woman had it handled. *I didn't want to interfere.*

However, when I was thinking this, I didn't hear *interfere*. I heard *enter fear*. Oh, yes. Now, I could see everything so much more clearly!

I finished paying for my dog treats and walked straight over to the woman. I set my bag down on the floor and asked, "Can I help?"

This *meltdown* was an emergency medical situation. Everyone was staring, but no one was helping.

The brave woman was the young boy's mom, and she let me know right away that he had type 1 diabetes and needed sugar *fast*. She was trying to hold him close so she could pour juice into his mouth. His flailing arms kept knocking everything from her hand. She quickly moved from juice to candy. She worked furiously to unwrap sugary candies to put into her son's mouth.

I wasn't sure he would let me hold him, but I offered to try so that his mom could focus. I took that child in my arms and immediately started praying and declaring peace. And you know what? Mom grabbed hold of that peace first. "Oh, thank you. Yes, let's pray." She joined me and started speaking blessings over her son. We both shifted to praying in tongues.

Where only the whites of his eyes had initially been visible, the young boy was now showing improvement. His eyes were attempting to focus, though he was still fighting, thrashing, and gasping for air. Three-year-olds are more robust than they look! Well-intentioned people came by to offer stickers to distract him.

Stickers! Store employees offered stickers instead of medical care. I guess it did sort of look like a tantrum, but it was so much more than that. And clearly, this wasn't mom's first time handling a situation like this. She was a champion!

We kept praying in tongues quietly over her son. When he calmed down, I asked Mom if I could pray for his healing. She said, "I didn't really know why we came into the store today, but it must have been for this." I agreed with her it must have been a divine appointment because it was the fourth store I had been to that afternoon for dog treats!

I told her I would pray for his complete healing. Still, she shouldn't stop any medications until a doctor advised her— that's what we learned to say at the healing conference. Only the person who prescribed the medication has permission to start, stop, or change that prescription.

In Jesus' name, I prayed to cast out the spirit of diabetes. I commanded a new pancreas into his body and for any damaged body parts to be healed and made whole. I blessed him and said, "Thank You, Jesus." That's all there was to it.

That's when Mom asked if I would pray for her daughter. "His seven-year-old sister is right here. She has the same thing.

Would you pray for her, too?" Big Sister had been standing quietly by the shopping cart the whole time. With all the commotion, I hadn't noticed her until that moment.

This child was so beautiful. I kneeled to speak to her face-to-face and asked her if it would be okay for me to pray for Jesus to heal her. Mom listened closely and proudly interjected that her daughter had been baptized at vacation Bible school the previous summer. "Oh, then we both love Jesus," I said to the young girl, "and Jesus wants to heal you."

Diabetes is an issue with a malfunctioning pancreas. I'm not even sure where the pancreas is, but the Lord showed me I should put my hand on the girl's back. At that moment, my hand felt on fire! When I opened my mouth to talk with her about what she might be feeling, I was incredibly overwhelmed by the love of Jesus. How do you put that into words? I started shaking, and I wanted to laugh and cry at the same time!

People were walking past slowly, watching and listening. Still, no one else stopped—and no store employees ever stepped forward to check on this family. After I prayed for the children, I prayed with Mom and spoke blessings over her.

Tears were flowing for both of us. My hands were shaking like crazy. She was praising Jesus, and so was I. We were having church right there in the checkout lanes!

Driving home, I pondered how God can move so unexpectedly, so swiftly, so wholly, wherever and whenever we yield ourselves to Him. I was incredibly humbled. It took me a full hour to stop shaking! It revved me up on the inside with holy reverence and awe.

The prompting to get involved was so very slight. It would have been easy to dismiss. Errands had taken a lot longer than I initially expected. I could have gone home after the third store, but then there was that *thought* to just stop by this one other store. Was that my thought, or was that the voice of the Lord? It's hard to say sometimes. It's so subtle.

It would have been easy to miss the quietness of His voice saying, *You know what to do.* There could have been a no at any point along the way, but God had other plans for this sweet young family. They were open to receiving from the Lord through *me* because the Lord will use the unlikeliest of people, won't He? Thank You, Jesus!

As a follow–up, I'd like to add that the pancreas is located in the abdomen, and pancreatic symptoms often manifest as pain in the belly or back. I know this because I looked it up online after I got home! My ignorance about human physiology has never disqualified me from praying for healing—or hindered God from moving to heal anyone I've prayed with.

Growing in Obedience

We are learning to walk in complete and total obedience to God, and for most Christians, this does not happen overnight. Apart from the Holy Spirit's power and ability to train us up in the way we should go, it would be impossible for us to live our lives fully obedient to God.

We have free will to say *no* to the Lord, but we risk enduring pain and loss of consciousness of God's presence (Song of Songs 5:6). There's more to it than that, though. We have opened ourselves up to sin when we say *no* to God and *yes* to God's enemy. Doing so gives the devil legal access to inhabit us and work through us to produce spiritual death (Ephesians 5:11, James 1:21, Romans 8:13).

Have we considered that it's for our good that we must be trained in obedience? God withholds no good thing from His children (Psalm 84:11). If we believed this, why would we ever choose disobedience? His boundaries keep us safe, and we can trust that His love never fails (1 Corinthians 13:8).

Perhaps obedience is something we learn progressively as well (Matthew 16:24, Hebrews 12:10–11). Our obedience to God starts with small things (Zechariah 4:10). In my own life, obedience training began curiously, and quite literally, with trash.

A few years ago, when the Lord put it in my heart to get a dog. I thought the dog was for my son, but she grew rather attached to me instead. Before this, I could have walked around my neighborhood on my own, but I didn't. Having a dog changed my routine, and I started walking through the neighborhood at different times of the day and night. As I walked the dog, I found that I could hear the Lord's voice with increased clarity.

The Lord taught me to intercede in prayer for families, businesses, communities, and governments on these routine outings. He also directed me to pick up trash. Whatever was left on the sidewalks or in the streets suddenly became my responsibility. One day as I was walking the dog through the neighborhood closest to home, I walked right past a crumpled-up fast-food bag that someone from a passing car had tossed aside. The voice of God rebuked me, saying, "You know you saw that."

Honestly, I was tired of picking up other people's trash, and I could hear myself responding aloud, "That's not mine. I didn't put it there." I kept walking, but the conviction was too great. I should have stopped to pick up the trash when I first saw it. Instead, I had to retrace my steps half a block to go back and pick it up. The Lord was right. I had seen the trash, and I knew I was supposed to pick it up. My disobedience was a sin, and it revealed just how much of *self* I was still listening to (Galatians 5:24–25).

Sometimes the thing that stands in our way of prospering is—us. God tells us if we stop pursuing our own desires, serving our own interests, and speaking empty words, then we will find joy as we serve Yahweh God. He will cause us to prosper (Isaiah 58:13–14 TPT). What if the speed of our obedience regulated our spiritual growth?

I'm finding that God often asks of us what is beyond our reach to accomplish on our own. It's not to frustrate us, but to stretch us beyond our comfort zone because the Lord desires for us to grow in faith to trust in Him (Matthew 19:26). Parents understand as young children grow, expectations often grow, too. The same is true in our relationship with Father God. As the Lord continues to grow us into the fullness of spiritual maturity, things that were once permissible might no longer be allowed. We can no longer get by with certain things. The Lord will correct those He loves (Proverbs 3:12, Hebrews 12:6).

Faith is active—it's not just a confession. As we grow in obedience to God, our life becomes increasingly hidden with Christ (Colossians 3:3 WEB, 2 Corinthians 4:8–11 WEB). Are we willing to be made invisible so that God's glory shines through us (2 Corinthians 4:7 TLB), or do we seek the approval of men (John 12:43)?

The journal entries I shared in chapter 5 highlighted areas where my faith still wavered. It exposed a cycle of being tossed back and forth—my response to the Lord being both *yes* and *no.* This up-and-down cycle revealed areas ruled by partial truths and outright lies. Confusion is not from God (1 Corinthians 14:33 NKJV), and neither is fear, impatience, frustration, apprehension, or rebellion. These are characteristics of occult bondage and influence.[5]

Listening to worldly reason and logic will not produce miracles. We must be resolute in our decision to follow Christ and remain steadfast in our declaration that Jesus is the Lord over all. How do we guard against occultism? The Lord invites us to stay focused on Him alone, and He says that when we do this, we'll have perfect peace.

> You will guard him *and* keep him in
> perfect *and* constant peace whose
> mind [both its inclination and its
> character] is stayed on You, because

he commits himself to You, leans on
You, *and* hopes confidently in You.
(Isaiah 26:3 AMPC)

Growing in spiritual maturity requires continual pressing in
and drawing nearer to God. Worldly pressures invite us to
give up and quit, but if we persevere and remain steadfast in
our faith, we will indeed walk in the victory and blessings of
the Lord.

Fully satisfied *and* assured that God
was able *and* mighty to keep His
word *and* to do what He had
promised. (Romans 4:21 AMPC)

Be sure to use the abilities God has
given you through his prophets when
the elders of the church laid their
hands upon your head. Put these
abilities to work; throw yourself into
your tasks so that everyone may
notice your improvement and
progress. Keep a close watch on all
you do and think. Stay true to what

is right and God will bless you and
use you to help others. (1 Timothy
4:14–16 TLB)

My friend, some days you may get everything right, while
other days, you may feel like you've wavered, failed or fallen.
I encourage you to get back up and dust yourself off
(Proverbs 24:16 TPT). Keep your mind and eyes on King
Jesus. From that place of abiding with Him, our nature is
transformed (John 15:4). The goal of life is not "not sinning"
(John 5:14, 8:11). The goal is to live in the presence and love
of Jesus (Psalms 27:4).

I don't want to be a better version of myself—ruling the life
of the flesh. I want Jesus to reign and rule my life by His love
and light. When we have a more profound revelation and
understanding of our true identity as children of God—as
kings and priests—we then adopt *His ways* as superior in
every area of life (Revelation 1:4–6 TLB). Father God first
expands His Kingdom within us and then fills us to
overflowing as He leads us to expand His Kingdom on earth.
It's our work as disciples to go and make more disciples
(Matthew 28:19–20 NKJV).

For those who live according to the
flesh set their minds on the things of
the flesh, but those *who live*
according to the Spirit, the things of
the Spirit. For to be carnally minded

is death, but to be spiritually minded *is* life and peace. Because the carnal mind *is* enmity against God; for it is not subject to the law of God, nor indeed can be. So then, those who are in the flesh cannot please God. But you are not in the flesh but in the Spirit, if indeed the Spirit of God dwells in you. Now if anyone does not have the Spirit of Christ, he is not His. And if Christ *is* in you, the body is dead because of sin, but the Spirit is life because of righteousness. (Romans 8:5–10 NKJV)

Corrections from God and Others

God continues to challenge my thinking, and I'm grateful for it. We receive correction from God's word, but also in community and fellowship with others. Our will is the spring of all our actions, but placing our will in God's hands produces triumph. Transitioning from thinking, saying, and doing things in our own strength to doing so in God's strength by fastening our faith to Him alone will feel uncomfortable.

Uncomfortableness simply recognizes that we've stepped out in faith, and we're depending on God, our Comforter, to direct our steps and carry us through to the other side. It's the Spirit of Holiness that comforts us with His presence (John 14:16), guides us into all truth (16:13), reminds us of God's word (14:26), testifies concerning Christ (15:26), and convicts the world of sin (16:7–8).

We know we are commissioned to heal the sick and that Jesus healed all who came to Him (Matthew 10:8, 15:30). Jesus said we would do even greater miracles than He did (John 14:12–14). If we're going to fulfill the Great Commission, we must know our identity and authority. We must also have faith to believe that God's word is true, alive, and full of power (Hebrews 4:12 AMPC). Then, it's only a matter of making ourselves available to go and do what God is calling us to do! What happens next is up to God!

Now, you may think that healing and miracles are the greatest gifts from God, but they're not. I have prayed for the gifts of healings (1 Corinthians 12:9, 28 NKJV), and I have devoted many hours and years to stewarding these gifts. Still, the Lord recently corrected a wrong perception regarding His gifts. It brings me to where I am today—still growing in the Lord and the fullness of spiritual maturity (Proverbs 3:5–6 NKJV). It was a lesson that brought tears and greater focus—and it all happened at a local grocery store.

Even when I don't need groceries for myself, if I feel God leading me to stop by the grocery store, I'll go. I picked up a few things on this day, and as I stood in the checkout lanes, I noticed an elderly couple in line behind me. What I did for them was nice, but what they did for me was priceless. I helped to meet their temporary need—they reminded me of eternal truth.

They stopped to talk with me as they moved toward the exit. I noticed the man had something going on with his eye, and I felt the Lord prompting me to ask him if there was anything I might ask Jesus to do for him. That's not usually how I ask people if I can pray with them, but that's what I asked. I thought the man would say he wanted his eye healed. However, that's not what he said at all. Without hesitation, he responded, "I would ask Jesus to use me to save another soul today."

I don't meet very many die-hard evangelists like this! Honestly, I can't say that I've ever met anyone who responded in this way—which is sad. Usually, people ask for new knees or some kind of physical healing—and that's very exciting— but this was far bigger. God had been encouraging me to pray bigger for years. *Is this what He meant?*

I thought I was stopping at the store to bless some folks, but it turns out I received the greater blessing. My eyes started leaking a steady stream of tears as the Lord's heart was revealed so spontaneously. Perhaps that's what prompted them to stay longer. They recounted several testimonies of God's goodness and faithfulness in their own lives. Hearing their testimonies was refreshing—like drinking straight from the fountain of Living Water (Revelation 21:6 TPT).

It had been far too long since I felt the same measure of God's presence in a church, but being filled by the Spirit at the grocery store wasn't the least bit awkward. And unlike some other venues, no one was looking for personal accolades or filming it all for marketing or fundraising efforts.

This man's unexpected response brought great conviction and correction. Indeed, the last several years have been a phenomenal journey of walking in faith to pray with others as God leads. I have been an eyewitness to many miraculous healings and shared innumerable prophetic words—but I'm inconsistent with purposely asking God to use my life to save souls.

In John 17, Jesus prays to the Father on behalf of the disciples.

> I have revealed to them who you are
> and I will continue to make you even
> more real to them, so that they may
> experience the same endless love
> that you have for me, for your love
> will now live in them, even as I live
> in them! (John 17:26 TPT)

It's our Great Commission to "go into all the world and preach the gospel to every creature" (Mark 16:15 NKJV). *Had I skipped this portion of scripture and focused on the signs, casting out demons, speaking with new tongues, and laying hands on the sick to see them recover (Mark 16:17–18 NKJV)?* The Lord's miracles are not to be discounted, but Jesus said that our true source of joy is that our names are registered as citizens of Heaven (Luke 10:20 TLB). The saving of souls (i.e., salvation) is the greatest miracle because it brings resurrection life—which is eternal.

But listen—that's not the point.
Don't be elated that evil spirits leave
when you say to leave. Rejoice that
your names are written in heaven.
(Luke 10:20 VOICE)

The gospel is the power of God to save every person who
would believe in Him (Romans 1:16 VOICE), yet, how will
they hear of Him unless we open our mouths to speak of
Him? We work in partnership with the Holy Spirit to share
the good news with others (Colossians 1:19–20). What an
honor to introduce others to Jesus!

Often, the Lord stretches our faith as He invites us to walk
more closely with Him. Just as Abraham had faith to believe
in God's leading, we, too, "through the Spirit eagerly wait for
the hope of righteousness by faith" (Galatians 5:5 NKJV). It
will cost us something, but there will be eternal rewards if we
don't grow weary. It's God who touches men's hearts to draw
them to Him. Still, He often invites us to be the voice, hands,
and feet of Christ. He has commissioned us to be fishers of
men (Mark 1:17 NKJV) who also go into all the world to
make disciples (Matthew 28:19–20 NKJV).

Continually Growing Toward Righteousness of Obedience

I believe the righteousness of faith and confidence in the Lord
leads us to the righteousness of obedience. There was a shift
that took place in my own life, and I suspect there will be for

your life as well. God's love draws us near to Him, but as we draw near to Him, He also draws near to us (James 4:8). It's like a divine dance. Our nearness to God requires separation from all else. This drawing nearer to God leaves us no longer content with a casual form of Christianity, enjoying a friendly yet distant relationship with the Lord. As we grow in our love for God, *that* love moves us to serve Him and to serve others (John 13:34–35).

As we mature in our relationship with God, it becomes our delight to do His will (Psalm 40:8). Indeed, we are united as one in Christ (John 17:22–23), and we long to fulfill all that He commissions of us because it is our joy, privilege, and honor to do so. We purpose to respond without hesitation to every opportunity the Lord lovingly sets before us as we follow Christ's example. Jesus' love for Father God guided His decisions (Luke 22:42, Matthew 11:27). As disciples of Jesus, we're learning from Him in the same ways the original disciples did. We know from scripture that Jesus' primary ministry on earth was not healing and miracles—it was the saving of souls (John 6:39).

> All of this is *a gift* from *our Creator* God, who has *pursued us and* brought us into a restored *and healthy* relationship with Him through the Anointed. And He has given us *the same mission*, the ministry of reconciliation, *to bring*

> *others back to Him. It is central to*
> *our good news that* God was in the
> Anointed making things right
> between Himself and the world. This
> means He does not hold their sins
> against them. But it also means He
> charges us to proclaim the message
> that heals and restores our broken
> relationships *with God and each*
> *other.* (2 Corinthians 5:18–19
> VOICE)

Eternal salvation is the greatest gift of all! Not only do we have the privilege of reconciling others to God, but we also have the honor of discipling others to help them mature in Christ. Being a Christian is 24/7. It's not limited to Sunday morning church service, and we must stop living like it is. I didn't have an immediate download or automatic understanding of God or His Kingdom when I got saved. I've never known anyone who did, though I know all things are possible for God.

My development as a Christian was delayed until God started connecting me with mentors, accountability partners, and spiritual mothers—people interested in spending time with me outside of church. The goal of salvation is not to fill empty seats in a church building but to fill empty people with the love of Christ. God wants us to be a part of His Kingdom and part of His family.

The world is watching and listening to all we do and say, and we have an opportunity for our lives to be a testimony of God's love (2 Corinthians 3:3). For most of us, our assignment for serving God takes place within our families, communities, and jobs—wherever we live our lives.

We are continually being transformed into Christ's image (Romans 8:29–30, Ephesians 4:13, Philippians 3:21). It's safe for us to follow God's voice when it's in harmony with His word, will, ways, nature, and character. If there's ever a time when we're unsure of how to proceed, we need only to look to the Bible to see what God has to say. We can ask God to clarify His will through His written word and trust that He will make it plain to us by the power of His Holy Spirit (James 1:5–6, John 14:26).

We use our God-given common sense, enlightened by the Holy Spirit, which also should align and harmonize with scripture. We are not opening our own doors, but it is the Lord who goes before us to open doors (2 Corinthians 2:12, Isaiah 22:22), and we are following in His steps (John 10:4).

I am able to do nothing from Myself [independently, of My own accord— but only as I am taught by God and as I get His orders]. Even as I hear, I judge [I decide as I am bidden to decide. As the voice comes to Me, so I give a decision], and My judgment is right (just, righteous), because I do not seek *or* consult My own will [I have no desire to do what is pleasing to Myself, My own aim, My own purpose] but only the will *and* pleasure of the Father Who sent Me. (John 5:30 AMPC)

I am not the same person I once was; still, I am not yet fully matured in Christlikeness. Dear friend, if you have joined me in this journey of reflection, I dare say that you, too, have grown in oneness with God—to look not only to His eyes but *through* His eyes at the world around you. Also, that you have been challenged, as I have, to say and do all that the Lord asks of us (John 2:5 WEB).

The Lord is always with us and longs to take full possession of the vessels He has created us to be—to be used by Him in any way He sees fit (2 Timothy 2:21–22). It's a journey that begins with a "yes," "I do," and "I will" to our Bridegroom King. Curious to know more about evangelism? Keep reading!

What Does God Say About This Topic?

Sing to the LORD, all the earth; Proclaim the good news of His salvation from day to day. (1 Chronicles 16:23 NKJV)

But the love of God will be perfected within the one who obeys God's Word. We can be sure that we've truly come to live in *intimacy with* God, not just by saying, "I am intimate with God," but by walking in the footsteps of Jesus. Beloved, I'm not writing a new commandment to you, but an old one that you had from the beginning, and you've already heard it. Yet, in a sense, it is a new commandment, as its truth is made manifest both in Christ and in you, because the darkness is disappearing and the true light is already blazing. (1 John 2:5–8 TPT)

But be doers of the word, and not hearers only, deceiving yourselves. For if anyone is a hearer of the word and not a doer, he is like a man observing his natural face in a mirror; for he observes himself, goes away, and immediately forgets what kind of man he was. (James 1:22–24 NKJV)

The fruit of the righteous is a tree of life. He who is wise wins souls. (Proverbs 11:30 WEB)

Application Challenge

Everything is an opportunity to serve God and serve others (Galatians 5:13). What if our ordinary daily tasks were done *in* Christ and *with* Christ—all for His glory? Would this change anything? Journal and ask, "Jesus, I recommit my life to your purposes. How can I serve You and show You honor? How can I serve and show honor to others?"

God's love expresses itself uniquely through you and your gifts. How does this look in your life?

Ask yourself what your life might look like if you didn't have to hold back anymore. Has the Lord invited you to start something new? Have you started what God has asked of you but not finished yet? Integrity is keeping your word to God and others by completing what you've started (Matthew 5:37).

If evangelism is of interest to you, you might enjoy Scott McNamara's book, *Jesus at the Door: Evangelism Made Easy*.

Let's Pray

Father God, we thank You for all Your words of wisdom. Lord, deliver us from all rebelliousness. Our trust is in You, God, and not in an arm of flesh. We purpose to do all that You command of us. Lord, establish Yourself in our hearts and minds. Strengthen us to stand with You and not bend or bow to the demands or temptations of Your enemy. Lord, we purpose to love You with all our heart, soul, mind, and strength, and to love others as much as we love ourselves (Mark 12:30–31 TLB). Lord, make our voices as loud as shofars to announce Your coming (Matthew 3:3), and echo Your love and Lordship throughout the earth.

Direct our steps, and strengthen us on our journey. Lord, thank You for the gift of transparency, which allows others to see You at work within us. Thank You, Holy Spirit, that Yours is the power by which we can accomplish all that You ask or require of us (Ephesians 3:20), and that it's all for God's eternal glory. It's in Jesus' Name we pray. Amen.

Chapter Eight

Basics of Evangelism and Practical Applications

God is not limited by time. I believe there has been a beautiful God-inspired destiny prepared for each of His children since before time began. It's no accident that we live in the age, time, and location we're living in.

> And He has made from one blood every nation of men to dwell on all the face of the earth, and has determined their preappointed times and the boundaries of their dwellings, so that they should seek the Lord, in the hope that they might grope for Him and find Him, though He is not far from each one of us; for in Him we live and move and have

our being, as also some of your own poets have said, "For we are also His offspring." (Acts 17:26–28 NKJV)

The Lord's love for us is without measure. His divine interventions mark us in unique and memorable ways. I believe the Lord called me to the International House of Prayer (IHOPKC) in Kansas City, Missouri, in 2016, for a season of alignment and restoration. It's where I first learned the importance of hearing His voice with clarity.

There, I learned to sit at the feet of Jesus. In *You Can Hear the Voice of God Through All Your Spiritual Senses,* I shared how my journey into healing and deliverance ministry began at the hands of children (Psalm 8:1–2). I marveled when a young girl spoke a powerful prophetic word to me. It spurred me to jealousy! *Would the Lord use me in that same way?* Perhaps you've wondered this, too, for your own life.

For too long, my voice had been silent regarding my faith in God. One afternoon, as I sat in the prayer room, I considered the many members of Christ's Body and their different roles and functions. On my way out, I noticed a flier advertising a weekly evangelism meeting. I thought, *I'm no evangelist, but evangelists are the voice of the Body. Maybe I'll check out their meeting and find out what evangelists are saying.* Are you curious to know what these meetings were like?

When Evangelists Gather

It was hardly different from any other meeting taking place on the IHOPKC campus. Meetings opened in worship and prayer. The group leader or special guest speaker shared a brief message and a word of exhortation. They encouraged those attending to share testimonies of outreach. Doing so demonstrated accountability, and it wonderfully glorified and honored the Lord. Questions were answered, upcoming outreach opportunities were shared, and the meetings ended with a closing prayer.

Meeting attendance varied based on the day and time and ranged from a handful of folks to upward of forty or more. The number of people attending never surprised me. Still, rather curiously, the meetings were primarily attended by those I considered introverts or less outgoing extroverts. I felt strangely welcome there, and I enjoyed hearing the testimonies of all that God was doing.

I met with an outreach group on Saturday mornings at 7:00 a.m. We partnered with different churches in the downtown area to serve breakfast at a local shelter. We started the day with a short Bible message and blessing. After that, we might sit at the tables talking and praying with others or head over to the resource center to help distribute food and clothes. Evangelism involved ministering to the genuine physical and emotional needs of others, and connecting others to Christ as we prayed for healing or salvation.

For several weeks, I also volunteered with a group on evening outreaches. We gathered under an overpass near the railroad tracks at a regularly scheduled time. The church we teamed up with provided a keyboard and worship leader. A brief message from scripture was shared and always followed with an invitation to receive salvation *and* pizza! We fed natural and spiritual hunger as we served others and showed honor to the people who made up that community. We weren't starting something new. We partnered with others where God was already working, which produced consistent good fruit.

I found it more challenging to connect with outreach groups after I returned home. When I invited others to join me, most didn't share my enthusiasm. Undeterred, I continued learning more about healing ministry and practicing listening for the Lord's directions. If your church doesn't offer opportunities for organized evangelism outreach, keep searching. Ask God to connect you with others who share an interest in serving. The needs are significant but often not communicated efficiently.

I was glad to partner with a local church near my home. Joining their group for evangelism outreach always blessed me. We would start our day by gathering at the church for prayer. From there, we drove to a large convalescent center, where we split into teams.

Without fail, every time I partner with others in ministry, the Lord uses our unique gifts to make the outreach both effortless and joyful. Here, to my great relief, a man on our team had a real knack for sharing the gospel with others. He shined in the loving way he boldly asked, "Do you know Jesus as your Lord and Savior?" His soft-spoken wife encouraged others sweetly by sharing testimony and prophecy. We were united in our belief that God still heals and performs miracles. Our prayers and declarations aligned with God's word. We didn't always see immediate results, though I believe these ministry outreaches were quite successful.

How do these shared experiences align with your views or experiences with evangelism? Somehow in my mind, I imagined evangelists were fanatical people hanging out on busy street corners. Perched atop old wooden soapboxes, they held an open Bible in one hand while pointing a finger of judgment at anyone who came near—all this while shouting messages about the end of the world. Where did this wrong image originate? Not from God, but perhaps this faulty perception prevented me from seeing myself as an evangelist.

Can people with quiet personalities be evangelists? Absolutely! I've seen it repeatedly! The one thing that seems to drive Christians into evangelism is a heart burning with passion for the Lord and an overwhelming desire to share the love of God with others.

Titles and Roles

The Lord has equipped us for His ministry's work. He has given "some to be apostles, some prophets, some evangelists, and some pastors and teachers," according to Ephesians 4:11 (NKJV). Strong's Greek Lexicon defines *evangelist* as "a preacher of the gospel" or someone who shares the good news of salvation through Christ.[6]

Before Jesus ascended into Heaven to take His place at the right hand of God, He directed His followers to "go into all the world and preach the gospel to every creature. He who believes and is baptized will be saved; but he who does not believe will be condemned. And these signs will follow those who believe: In My name they will cast out demons; they will speak with new tongues; they will take up serpents; and if they drink anything deadly, it will by no means hurt them; they will lay hands on the sick, and they will recover" (Mark 16:15–18 NKJV). He also said in verse 20, "And they went out and preached everywhere, the Lord working with *them* and confirming the word through the accompanying signs. Amen."

The Lord directed them to *go*, but He never instructed them to go alone. In this co-mission, He worked with them to confirm their words through miracles and other supernatural signs.

I hadn't considered how healing and evangelism might go hand in hand until just a few years ago. Mark 16 makes the expectation clear for all Christians. The demonstration of divine healing draws unbelievers to salvation in Christ. A Christian healing evangelist knows their identity as a child of God and knows their authority in Christ to see others healed and saved.

How many times had I read these familiar verses and thought they were for others? When the Lord confronted me in 2015, He also rescued me from a decades-long lifestyle of passive Christianity. When He directed me to start a prayer group in my home, I realized how unprepared I was. When He compelled me to lead others in communion, my inexperience in this area was undoubtedly apparent to everyone. Still, the Lord wasn't threatened by my ignorance or immaturity. Instead, He taught me (and others in the group) to trust His voice as He directed us week after week. God showed His commitment to teaching us His ways.

> But the manifestation of the Spirit is given to each one for the profit *of all*: for to one is given the word of wisdom through the Spirit, to another the word of knowledge through the same Spirit, to another faith by the same Spirit, to another gifts of healings by the same Spirit, to another the working of miracles, to another prophecy, to another discerning of spirits, to another *different* kinds of tongues, to another the interpretation of tongues. But one and the same Spirit works all these things, distributing to each one individually as He wills. (1 Corinthians 12:7–11 NKJV)

I believe the gifts of healings and other manifestations of the Spirit mentioned in 1 Corinthians 12:7–11 are available to all born-again, Spirit-filled believers in Christ. Stepping out in faith and obedience as the Lord leads puts us in a position to see these gifts manifested according to the needs set before us.

Sharing God's Love with Others

Do you think God can't use you for this kind of ministry because you don't have special training in these areas? I used to think that, too. I haven't been to seminary and have had no formal religious training. Perhaps the Lord uses me as a sign that makes people wonder! God uses untrained men and women. As with Moses, Elisha, Gideon, and others, the Lord is not looking at our résumé; He's looking for our Yes. God has repeatedly proven He equips those He calls (Exodus 4:10–11, 1 Kings 19:19, Judges 7:2).

But God chose the foolish things of the world to shame the wise. He chose the weak things of the world to shame the strong. And he chose what the world thinks is not important. He chose what the world hates and thinks is nothing. He chose these to destroy what the world thinks is important. God did this so that no man can brag before him. It is God who has made you part of Christ Jesus. Christ has become wisdom for us from God. Christ is the reason we are right with God and have freedom from sin; Christ is the reason we are holy. So, as the

> Scripture says, "If a person brags, he should brag only about the Lord." (1 Corinthians 1:27–31 ICB)

When Peter and John spoke to the lame beggar sitting at the Gate Beautiful, they ministered to him in a way that brought very different "change," and all the people marveled (Acts 3:1–10). As a result, Peter and John were arrested and brought before the rulers and elders to explain themselves.

> Now when they saw the boldness of Peter and John, and perceived that they were uneducated and untrained men, they marveled. And they realized that they had been with Jesus. (Acts 4:13 NKJV)

Acts 4:13 (NLT) says, "For they could see that they were ordinary men with no special training in the Scriptures." Oh, how that verse fills me with hope! How did Peter and John respond when they were released and ordered not to speak of Jesus again? When they returned to the other believers and shared what had happened, all the people rejoiced and prayed to God for boldness to continue sharing the power of His words with others (Acts 4:23–31).

Peter and John were both disciples of Christ. We also know they were apostles. Didn't they preach messages and teach others about Jesus? Didn't they also prophesy, pray to heal the sick, and evangelize? Perhaps when the Lord equips us for "every good work" (2 Timothy 3:17 NKJV), He's simply looking for people who will say yes and trust Him with the rest. The Lord will activate all we will need to accomplish all He asks of us (1 Corinthians 12:11 TPT).

The disciples stepped out in faith to go, say, and do all God led them to. The path they chose was undeniably difficult, yet they purposed to go that way without excuse. Ephesians 4:11 (NKJV) tells us God "gave some *to be* apostles, some prophets, some evangelists, and some pastors and teachers" to equip the saints for the work of ministry. What if the "some" Christ gave was *you*? Indeed, what the Lord empowered Peter, John, and all the other disciples to do, He will empower us to do, too—if only we would believe Him for it.

I'll tell you from experience—the most challenging part is taking that first step of faith! Throughout this series, I've openly shared fears, doubts, and wrong mindsets for a reason. I understand the internal struggle you may feel, but I also know firsthand how strong the Lord is to help us break free of enemy strongholds.

Healing by itself is not the gospel; instead, it's a tool we use to preach the gospel to win souls to Christ. Have you considered that now is the only time we will ever have to step into the role of an evangelist? Today is the day of creative miracles, healing, and resurrection power. The people we meet in Heaven will have already received the gift of eternal salvation and also their immortal, glorified bodies (1 Corinthians 15:51–53). There will be no need to use the gifts of miracles, healing, or evangelism for those living in

Heaven. Our window of opportunity is limited to this short-lived lifetime on earth (Psalm 78:39, 103:15–17).

We're serving the Lord as we love and care for our families and communities. We're honoring and serving the Lord when we put others first. That may look like buying groceries for a family in need or allowing someone to move ahead of you in the checkout line at the store. It may look like calling a friend and offering to pray, or sending a friend a letter of encouragement in the mail. What if these little things counted as evangelism? We extend the same love and care we would extend to our family members because we are all one family in Christ.

Ministers of Reconciliation

Every born-again Christian is a minister of reconciliation authorized to speak on Christ's behalf as an ambassador of Heaven's Kingdom (2 Corinthians 5:18–21). The Passion Translation clarifies the matter, saying, "We are the voice of heaven to the earth, invested with royal power through the name of Jesus and authority of his blood" (2 Corinthians 5:20, footnote).

Asking others if they know Jesus Christ as their Savior and Lord can feel awkward at first. Still, there's good fruit to be harvested for those willing to go out on a limb. Evangelism is a co-mission since God is always with us (Hebrews 13:5). It's His will that none would perish but that all would come to Him in repentance (2 Peter 3:9 NLV), avoiding eternal punishment.

As Spirit-filled believers in Christ, we're carefully listening for God's guidance. We're learning to walk in immediate obedience as we say and do all that He asks or requires of us to demonstrate His Kingdom of Heaven on earth (Romans 15:18–19, John 17:10 TPT).

> Heal the sick, raise the dead, cure those with leprosy, and cast out demons. Give as freely as you have received! (Matthew 10:8 NLT)

How do we do this? As God leads, it's often as simple as asking, "May I pray for you?" When you've received God's miracle healing in your own body, it gives you a testimony and launches you into evangelism! How easy it is to say, "Excuse me. It looks like you're experiencing some pain. I used to have _____, too, and then God healed me. I've seen others healed as I've prayed for them. Would you mind if I pray and ask God to heal you?"

God is our Healer (Exodus 15:26). When healing comes, it opens a door. Christ has entrusted us with the ministry of "opening the door of reconciliation to God" (2 Corinthians 5:19 TPT). Opening a door for someone is easy. As born-again, Spirit-filled believers in Christ, miracle signs follow us everywhere we go (Mark 16:17–18). We're on a rescue mission, inviting others to be translated out of the kingdom of darkness (Colossians 1:13). We're pointing others to Jesus— the way, the truth, and the life (John 14:6 WEB).

Salvation Simplified

We were all born into a fallen world of sin ruled by the god of this age (2 Corinthians 4:4 NKJV). The fruit of sin is death and separation from God. In Romans 3:23 (NLT), we read, "For everyone has sinned; we all fall short of God's glorious standard." We cannot redeem ourselves, and no amount of striving or personal sacrifice can earn salvation. The good news is that Jesus Christ has paid our sin debt in full and paved the way for us to be reconciled back to Father God (Matthew 24:14).

> [All] are justified *and* made upright *and* in right standing with God, freely *and* gratuitously by His grace (His unmerited favor and mercy), through the redemption which is [provided] in Christ Jesus. (Romans 3:24 AMPC)

Without a Savior, we are spiritually dead, ruled by sin (Romans 3:9–12), and alienated from the life and love of God (Ephesians 4:17–18). Being a morally upright person and doing good works won't save us from spending an eternity in hell. Only Jesus can save us. If Jesus is not our Lord, we are following another leader, dictator, or lord. Through the ministry of evangelism, we're inviting others to leave the kingdom of darkness, death, and deceit ruled by Satan.

Whatever country you live in, you're ruled by the leader of that country, and the fruit of this decision is evident to others (Jeremiah 17:10, Galatians 5:22–23). We can choose to renounce our citizenship in the kingdom of darkness and elect to live as children of light in the Lord (Ephesians 5:8).

When we ask Jesus to be our Savior and Lord, we're saying we want to learn the ways of the Kingdom of God. This decision for spiritual redemption determines where we will dwell for eternity. Here on earth, we're living in a spiritual war zone where an invisible battle takes place all around us (Ephesians 6:12).

The first step is to recognize that we're being ruled by darkness. We confess we are sinners in need of saving and repent of our sins (Matthew 4:17). According to Acts 4:12 (ICB), "Jesus is the only One who can save people. No one else in the world is able to save us." Romans 10:9 (ICB) makes it simple, "If you declare with your mouth, 'Jesus is Lord,' and if you believe in your heart that God raised Jesus from death, then you will be saved." We believe and receive.

> For God so loved the world, that he gave his one and only Son, that whoever believes in him should not perish, but have eternal life. (John 3:16 WEB)

The Kingdom of God is about "living a life of goodness and peace and joy in the Holy Spirit" (Romans 14:17 NLT), but this doesn't mean we won't encounter obstacles in our journey. We enter a war when we become Christians (Matthew 11:11–12, 2 Corinthians 10:3–6 TPT).

I've found that although salvation is instant, sanctification is progressive (1 Thessalonians 5:23 NKJV). We're progressively walking in wholeness and holiness as we learn God's ways of thinking, speaking, and acting.

For this reason, I encourage you to disciple those you lead to salvation in Christ (Psalm 51:12–13). Loving relationships are important to God (John 13:34–35). Be intentional about setting new believers up for success. If you're not able to disciple them directly, connect them with others who can. New believers are hardly aware that they've been born again into a spiritual battlefield. Spiritual mothers and fathers committed to the discipleship process are an essential resource often missing in American churches.

Winning souls to Christ is our primary earth assignment. This doesn't mean we have to stand on street corners evangelizing in awkward ways (unless God directs us to do so). Neither does God call everyone to stand on a worldwide stage to lead others to Christ in the same way He used Billy Graham and Reinhard Bonnke. More likely, we'll minister to others a few at a time. In that case, we're able to show them the love of Christ by connecting with them. Following up to ask how they're doing is the loving thing to do. We do for others the same we would want them to do for us or our loved ones (Matthew 7:12 ICB).

If you mess up, fail, or fall, extend grace to yourself (Proverbs 24:16 TPT). Take the matter straight to God. Ask Him to strengthen you to walk in immediate obedience. Keep trying. You're doing God's will, and it's important.

Make Time for Debriefing or Processing

Government and military workers understand the importance of debriefing after an assignment. The debriefing process allows those deployed on a mission to share and ask questions to extend their learning. *What worked? What did we get right? What produced good fruit—and how can we replicate those results?* It's a time to download, process, and release everything that has just happened on the mission.

Debriefing is an essential yet often overlooked part of ministry.

Jesus sent His disciples out on mission in pairs or groups. When they returned, they met again with Him to report how the mission went. We can follow Christ's example.

> After these things the Lord appointed seventy others also, and sent them two by two before His face into every city and place where He Himself was about to go. (Luke 10:1 NKJV)

Then the seventy returned with joy, saying, "Lord, even the demons are subject to us in Your name." And He said to them, "I saw Satan fall like lightning from heaven. Behold, I give you the authority to trample on serpents and scorpions, and over all the power of the enemy, and nothing shall by any means hurt you. Nevertheless do not rejoice in this, that the spirits are subject to you, but rather rejoice because your names are written in heaven." In that hour Jesus rejoiced in the Spirit and said, "I thank You, Father, Lord of heaven and earth, that You have hidden these things from *the* wise and prudent and revealed them to babes. Even so, Father, for so it seemed good in Your sight. All things have been delivered to Me by My Father, and no one knows who the Son is except the Father, and who the Father is except the Son, and *the one*

to whom the Son wills to reveal
Him." Then He turned to *His*
disciples and said privately, "Blessed
are the eyes which see the things you
see; for I tell you that many prophets
and kings have desired to see what
you see, and have not seen *it*, and to
hear what you hear, and have not
heard *it*." (Luke 10:17–24 NKJV)

Being on a co-mission with Christ requires compassion and love for others. God will often activate our spiritual senses or provide us with new tools, revelations, or insights as we minister to others. God reveals His heart to those He trusts. Debriefing is not a matter of gossiping or bragging. It's about learning to work together to build up the Body of Christ.

Walking in the supernatural is not yet normal for most people. The debriefing process is helpful for both the care recipient and the ministry team. Debriefing aids in recovery and helps make future missions more successful.

Debriefing is such an excellent learning tool that even if you're not quite ready to go out on missions, you can still use this tool at the end of each day in your quiet time with God. You might ask, *Lord, what was Your favorite part of the day? What part went right? What part could have gone better?*

> Owe nothing to anyone except to
> love one another; for the one who
> loves his neighbor has fulfilled the
> Law. (Romans 13:8 NASB)

Learn from the positives and negatives. Take your responsibilities seriously, but have fun. We want our thoughts, words, attitudes, and actions to guide others back to Jesus. I pray you will consistently live in the truth of God's word and love others well.

For those unable to "go," your times of Spirit-led prayerful intercession are a power-filled essential for aligning and strengthening the Body. I'm often interceding for others in prayer as I take care of family, home, and business. In all things, we're learning to live God-centered lives!

What Does God Say About This Topic?

He has shown you, O man, what *is* good; And what does the Lord require of you But to do justly, To love mercy, And to walk humbly with your God? (Micah 6:8 NKJV)

The blind see and *the* lame walk; *the* lepers are cleansed and *the* deaf hear; *the* dead are raised up and *the* poor have the gospel preached to them. (Matthew 11:5 NKJV)

But you be watchful in all things, endure afflictions, do the work of an evangelist, fulfill your ministry. (2 Timothy 4:5 NKJV)

Therefore tongues are for a sign, not to those who believe but to unbelievers; but prophesying is not for unbelievers but for those who believe. (1 Corinthians 14:22 NKJV)

Only I can tell you the future before it even happens. Everything I plan will come to pass, for I do whatever I wish. (Isaiah 46:10 NLT)

If I am not doing the works [performing the deeds] of My Father, then do not believe Me [do not adhere to Me and trust Me and rely on Me]. But if I do them, even though you do not believe Me *or* have faith in Me, [at least] believe the works *and* have faith in what I do, in order that you may know and understand [clearly] that the Father is in Me, and I am in the Father [One with Him]. (John 10:37–38 AMPC)

Application Challenge

Let's be sure that our heart's motives are pure when we're ministering to the needs of others and speaking on behalf of Christ, our King. In 1 Peter 3:15 (NKJV), the apostle Peter encourages us to "always be ready to *give* a defense to everyone who asks you a reason for the hope that is in you." Have you considered what you might say to others? How would you answer if someone asked you why you believe in God?

Is your faith in Christ an everyday reality and necessity, or is it reserved for Sundays and emergencies? Jesus said He was returning soon (Revelation 22:12 NLT). If you thought He was returning next week, who would you want to share your faith with immediately?

As a Christian, you believe in Heaven, but do you also believe in hell? I encourage you to read or listen to Bill Wiese's testimony *23 Minutes In Hell: One Man's Story About What He Saw, Heard, and Felt in that Place of Torment.*

Let's Pray

Father God, we praise You. Thank You for calling us to You and pouring out your Spirit of Adoption (Romans 8:15) upon us to make us your sons and daughters. We purpose to wash daily in the water of Your word (Ephesians 5:26) to cleanse ourselves of every worldly defilement. Holy Spirit, thank You for Your presence and gifts. Guard us until our full salvation is ready to be revealed (1 Peter 1:5 TPT). Lord, we hold fast to our confession of hope, for You are faithful (Hebrews 10:23 NKJV). Help us consider others as we stir up love and good works within Your Body (Hebrews 10:24 NKJV).

Lord Jesus, nothing can stop You from reaching us, restoring us, helping us, and encouraging us. Kindle a holy boldness within us to enlarge Your Kingdom. You are the Lord of the harvest. We're asking for more workers in the field (Luke 10:2 NLT). We thank You for this time of great awakening, new beginnings, and for eternal revelation of who You are. It's in the magnificent Name of Jesus we pray. Amen.

Frequently Asked Questions

It's only by the power of the Holy Spirit within us we're able to accomplish the Great Commission to go into all the world and preach the gospel with miracles, signs, and wonders that follow (Mark 16:15–17 NKJV). The miracles, signs, and wonders are for unbelievers (John 4:48). I was an unbelieving "believer" for years, but when I finally came to my senses and turned back to the Lord, I had a lot of questions! The Lord was faithful to answer my questions. As I share my testimony with others, people often ask similar questions.

How does it look for an ordinary Christian to walk in the supernatural? The first step to walking in the supernatural is believing that it's not only possible, but it's possible for *you*. Everyone who takes that first step will grow in strength and faith as they continue the journey. It all starts with time spent in the word and with the Word. After that first major hurdle, the following steps become easier. We're simply following Jesus' example to pray and listen, then to say and do all that God asks of us.

Can anyone do what you do? According to Mark 16:17–18, these signs *shall* follow every born-again, Spirit-filled believer in Christ. It's up to you to decide if you'll partner with God in this. We're all uniquely created in God's image and likeness, and the way God works out these miraculous signs will be a wonder to us all! There are many unique gifts for the Body of Christ. Because of our uniqueness, God's presence manifests in different ways.

Does God direct you to people to minister to them? Yes, He does. I'm finding that I don't have to go out of my way to find myself on the mission field. Wherever my feet step, that's my mission field. It's my family, home, business, neighborhood, community, church, the places I shop—all these are my mission field! Every job involves serving others no matter where we go or what we do. The Lord uses those who make themselves available. Within the boundaries of my mission field (Acts 5:12), the Lord directs me to whom He would have me minister (Acts 4:30). It's often such a subtle nudge that it would be easy to miss.

Does God have you go out of your way to help people? Sometimes He does, but more often not. Of course, I want my schedule to be His schedule. Still, many times, God simply directs me to minister to people who intersect my path as I go about taking care of routine daily tasks (Colossians 3:23–24, Matthew 20:26–28).

When you pray for someone to be healed, is their healing immediate or gradual? My job is to pray in alignment with whatever God is directing me to say or do. I'm listening to hear what God is saying, then I'm simply repeating His words, or I'm doing whatever He's showing me to do. In every case, it's up to God to heal in whatever way He decides. Healing may be immediate, gradual, or conditional. Each situation is unique.

Sometimes the person I'm praying with receives immediate miraculous healing. I can see or feel what God is doing to heal that person. Foolish words like "I know these things take time" or "I imagine I'll feel better in a few weeks" can negatively affect a person's healing. These silly kinds of statements are not scriptural. When Jesus healed, the results were immediate or required walking it out in faith (2 Kings 5:10, John 9:7).

> I tell you the truth: whoever believes
> in Me will be able to do what I have
> done, but they will do even greater
> things, because I will return to be
> with the Father. (John 14:12 VOICE)

Perhaps the better question here would be, "How will I respond when I pray according to God's word, but His promises don't manifest right away?" Sometimes, that's the actual test. Will it tempt me to walk away offended when the promise doesn't come according to my preferred timing? Or will I continue to fight for what God says is my inheritance? I was tested in this area with the left shoulder issue I mentioned in this book's introduction.

Will I stand in faith? Will I continue to press in? Will I ask that person if I can pray again—or again? There may be layers of deep-rooted strongholds or false belief systems to be addressed and brought down before a promise manifests in the physical realm. These harmful "weeds" must be removed to prepare the soil of our hearts to receive God's word (Matthew 13:3–30 TPT).

When you pray for someone to be healed, does it affect you? Yes, when I pray for others, it often affects me personally. When the Lord allows me to feel another person's pain in my body as a word of knowledge (1 Corinthians 12:8), I'm a lot more inclined to offer to pray!

Remember, we don't heal anyone, but we give all issues to God, our Healer. We're connecting people with God and praying in faith and expectancy to experience the right-now manifestation of God's promises. The Passion Translation tells us in 1 Corinthians 13:8, "Love remains long after *words of* knowledge are forgotten." Words of knowledge serve a temporary purpose, but love is eternal.

When I attended the conference on healing the sick in 2017, the meeting opened with extended worship, followed by reading scriptures about God's will to heal. Audience participation was encouraged, and age didn't matter. Young children were coming forward to pray with others, and we were seeing them healed!

When a young lady stood up and asked for prayer to be healed of cancer, I felt compassion toward her. She had just been released from the hospital and was still wearing a medical bracelet. Doctors had diagnosed her with the same type of cancer I had when I was in my twenties. I don't remember what I prayed. I simply agreed with her that this cancer wasn't from God, and it was His will to heal her body. As I spoke those words aloud, I physically felt the hand of God move upon my own body. It was both unexpected and supernaturally marvelous! I didn't know something like that was possible. I didn't "give to get," but God blessed and brought a more significant measure of healing to both of us that day.

I have shown you in every way, by laboring like this, that you must support the weak. And remember the words of the Lord Jesus, that He said, "It is more blessed to give than to receive." (Acts 20:35 NKJV)

Jesus said to her, "Did I not say to you that if you would believe you would see the glory of God?" (John 11:40 NKJV)

You must continually bring healing
to lepers and to those who are sick,
and make it your habit to break off
the demonic presence from people,
and raise the dead back to life.
Freely you have received *the power
of the kingdom*, so freely release it to
others. (Matthew 10:8 TPT)

Is it better for us to pray specific prayers or to speak general healing and blessings? Only God can say. That's why we ask Him how He would have us pray. Each situation and circumstance is different. You might start by considering what the Bible says about a topic. God has already spoken and given us His answer. Often, He's waiting for us to apply that word to our situation. By faith, we know that whatever we ask, according to God's will and word, He will do because He is faithful (1 John 5:14–15).

Do you have to be touching the person needing healing, or can it work over a distance? There are many kinds of healing gifts to meet all healing needs (1 Corinthians 12:30). Many people are healed by phone or video, with prayer cloths, or in large groups where it would be impossible to touch each person directly. In Matthew 8:5–13, Jesus sent His word to the centurion's household to heal the officer's servant. We send forth God's word, too, when we pray according to scripture. People were healed in the streets as Peter walked by

(Acts 5:14–16). We do not limit how God will bring healing, to whom, or when.

> So also will be the word that I speak;
> it does not return to me unfulfilled.
> My word performs my purpose and
> fulfills the mission I sent it out to
> accomplish. (Isaiah 55:11 TPT)

> God kept releasing a flow of
> extraordinary miracles through the
> hands of Paul. Because of this,
> people took Paul's handkerchiefs and
> articles of clothing, even pieces of
> cloth that had touched his skin,
> laying them on the bodies of the
> sick, and diseases and demons left
> them and they were healed. (Acts
> 19:11–12 TPT)

At this time, my beliefs about God differ from what I believed twenty years ago or even five years ago. I want to grow in spiritual maturity—I have grown, and I'm still growing! That's because I'm learning from God and His word daily—and my heart is open to correction.

They found that the Jews of Berea
were of more noble character and
much more open minded than those
of Thessalonica. They were hungry
to learn and eagerly received the
word. Every day they opened the
scrolls of Scripture to search and
examine them, to verify that what
Paul taught them was true. (Acts
17:11 TPT)

The Lord is gracious and merciful to confront us with His
truth. He is the "something more" that our souls innately
crave. As we awaken to our true identity and authority in
Christ, we grow, and we must be intentional about helping
others to grow as well.

Conclusion

Love God, Love Yourself, Love Others

Though we find ourselves at the end of this three-part series, our journey with God is eternal. Our Lord has a plan and purpose for each of us. It would be impossible to come to a fullness of spiritual maturity in faith outside of being a part of a Body of believers. We need each other. Everyone that we encounter helps us to grow, whether or not we realize it. Remember, even those who bring out the worst in us help us by revealing issues to be addressed, refined, or upgraded within ourselves.

> For his "body" *has been formed in his image* and is closely joined together and constantly connected as one. And every member *has been given divine gifts* to contribute to the growth of all; and as *these gifts* operate effectively throughout the

> whole body, we are built up and
> made perfect in love. (Ephesians
> 4:16 TPT)

Just as Jesus called for Peter to make it his life's mission to strengthen his brothers and feed God's sheep (John 21:17 NKJV), I believe God has challenged each of us in the same way. As we grow in intentionality to share our testimonies with others, it strengthens our faith and inspires us to keep moving forward.

> But I have prayed for you, Peter, that
> you would stay faithful to me no
> matter what comes. Remember this:
> after you have turned back to me and
> have been restored, make it your life
> mission to strengthen the faith of
> your brothers. (Luke 22:32 TPT)

My friend, there's a place of breakthrough that's well worth fighting to reach. Clarity and peace are for us as we dwell in our promised land. It requires positioning ourselves in God's presence until we're able to see from His perspective. Seeing through the lenses of God's heart changes everything.

I pray you will experience the world around you in these fresh ways as you grow into the fullness of all that God has called you to be. I pray you will continually strive to enter His rest

(Hebrews 4:11 NKJV) and that you'll learn to see yourself exactly as God sees you. Embrace the uniqueness of His purposes for your life, and continually be filled with His love and power.

Our commission is summed up in three parts: love God, love yourself, and love others (Matthew 22:37–40). Let me leave you with a few practical application steps for fulfilling the Lord's command.

Love God

Everything we know about God's nature is manifested in Jesus (John 14:9). Spending more time with God transformed my life. It helped me to grow in spiritual maturity and confidence in faith. Do yourself a favor and find a Bible that's easy for you to read and understand. Spend time with God in His word every day. On the days when you're time-crunched to sit still to read, try listening to the Bible on audio, app, CD, DVD, or video.

Develop your relationship with God by spending time with Him. That's where you'll come to know the fullness of the love He has for you. Talk to Him. Don't always go to God with a shopping list full of things you want from Him. Try asking Him how you can minister to Him. Ask Him what's on His heart, then ask Him how you can be a part of that.

Sing to God. Do you think that's unusual? King David sang to God. He wrote God poems and sang Him songs—we call them Psalms. God considered David a man after His heart! Read God's word back to Him. He loves to hear your voice!

Ask Him questions. Engage with Him. Make God the center of all things—then watch and see what kind of ripple effect it has on your life.

Love Yourself

Clarifying our view of God also brings clarity to how we view ourselves. Our most potent beliefs are what we believe about God and what we think about ourselves. Challenging our assumptions to establish truth in our lives is essential. While we can—and should—ask God questions, don't make the mistake of questioning God's love. Instead, let His truth be firmly established in your heart. Remember, if we wouldn't say it to God, we shouldn't say it about ourselves or others made in God's image.

Now is our time of preparation. We want to be good stewards of all that God has entrusted to us. We want to be ready for Jesus' return. He is coming back for a mature Bride. Risk putting yourself out there, looking foolish, and making mistakes. It's how you'll grow.

Love Others

Dare to invest in others. Focus on the truth of God's word. Spur one another on, build each other up and encourage each other. Do a new thing. If you feel it's safe, consider opening your hearts and homes for prayer meetings and Bible studies. Hold each other accountable. Having mentors and spiritual accountability helps us to grow.

I challenge you to be a disciple-maker. Be deliberate about investing in the spiritual development of others. Allow God to make these critical connections. Our goal is "that we may present everyone fully mature in Christ" (Colossians 1:28 NIV).

I may buy a book about exercise and read that book—but it won't change how my body looks unless I apply what I'm reading and activate my muscles. I must invest time using the book's principles to get the results. In the same way, I encourage you to stir up your faith (2 Timothy 1:6 NKJV) by exercising your spiritual muscles. Activate what you're learning and keep expanding the Kingdom of God by sharing and imparting what you're learning with others (Matthew 10:8 NKJV). There will be undeniable benefits for pursuing God single-mindedly and wholeheartedly.

Perhaps the most significant advantage is leaving a heritage of love. We can exchange twisted thoughts, false beliefs, and enemy strongholds for God's truth. Trading negative influences, patterns, and curses for generational blessings leaves a "Power full" legacy! The healing that comes from spending time with God affects our lives, the lives of those dear to us, our generation, and future generations.

Go after a life of love as if your life depended on it—because it does. Give yourselves to the gifts God gives you. Most of all, try to proclaim his truth. If you praise him in the private language of tongues, God understands you but no one else does, for you are sharing intimacies just between you and him. But when you proclaim his truth in everyday speech, you're letting others in on the truth so that they can grow and be strong and experience his presence with you. (1 Corinthians 14:1–3 MSG)

What Shall We Do Now?

What shall we do now? That's the question I heard as I interceded in prayer recently. Frequently, when the Lord prompts me to pray in my prayer language, I'll see pictures or visions of what's happening in the spirit realm. Regularly, too, He'll allow me to interpret words spoken in tongues. Often, I'll hear scripture references. In this instance, I heard, *Let's bless them with every good and perfect gift from the Father of lights above.* That's a reference to James 1:17. A smile erupted on my face.

I had been praying for all the children of the Lord. *Withhold no good thing,* I heard (Psalm 84:11). *To all,* came the command.

The Spirit of multiplication is poured out to bless all we set our hearts and hands to (Deuteronomy 15:10). *Your Spirit of*

Salvation is poured out upon the earth (1 Peter 1:5 TPT, Galatians 3:5).

> But he who endures to the end shall
> be saved. And this gospel of the
> kingdom will be preached in all the
> world as a witness to all the nations,
> and then the end will come.
> (Matthew 24:13–14 NKJV)

These hope-filled words encouraged me, and I pray they will inspire you as well. Friend, let's intentionally move forward with God into the fullness of all that He has purposed for us. After all the Lord has done for me, He still lovingly works within me to cause my temporal mindsets to shift toward eternity. He also challenges me to bring others with me as I continue growing into full awareness of who He is and who I am as His beloved child. Do you have people in your life you could invite to join you on your journey?

I believe each concept presented in this series was from the Lord and meant to restore and challenge us to receive the "more" He has for us. The foundational concepts of salvation and sharing our testimony were covered in book one of this series. We come full circle as we have applied these concepts to our lives and now step out in holy boldness to share these same principles with others. Kingdom expansion is first an inner work and builds outwardly. It also prepares us to take the next steps of sharing our gifts and resources with the world.

In the yearlong process of writing this series, the Lord taught me many new things, which I then shared with others—fresh Bread straight from Heaven's ovens. And though the Lord's corrections didn't feel good, they were for my eternal good and profitable for drawing many people nearer to Jesus. Dear friend, I trust the Lord would, will, and has already done the same for you! The Kingdom of God is ever-expanding (Luke 12:32), and so is our revelation of who God is! In all things, I pray God would "perfect, establish, strengthen, and settle you" for His eternal glory (1 Peter 5:10–11 NKJV). Amen.

Notes

Chapter 1

1. "G4991 – Sōtēria – Strong's Greek Lexicon (KJV)," Blue Letter Bible, accessed December 5, 2020, https://www.blueletterbible.org/lang/lexicon/lexicon.cfm?Strongs=G4991.

2. "G3341 – Metanoia – Strong's Greek Lexicon (KJV)," Blue Letter Bible, accessed January 9, 2020, https://www.blueletterbible.org/lang/lexicon/lexicon.cfm?Strongs=G3341.

Chapter 4

3. Lewis E. Jones, "Power in the Blood," Hymnary.org, accessed January 11, 2021, https://hymnary.org/text/would_you_be_free_from_the_burden_jones.

Chapter 6

4. "Apprehend," Merriam-Webster.com Dictionary, accessed November 15, 2020, https://www.merriam–webster.com/dictionary/apprehend.

Chapter 7

5. Henry Wright, A More Excellent Way, (New Kensington: Whitaker House, 2009), 264–265.

Chapter 8

6. "G2099 – euangelistēs – Strong's Greek Lexicon (NKJV)," Blue Letter Bible, accessed August 17, 2021, https://www.blueletterbible.org/lexicon/g2099/nkjv/tr/0–1/.

Bible Translations

Unless otherwise indicated, all Scripture quotations are sources from www.BibleGateway.com. This page is a continuation of the Copyright Page.

Scripture quotations taken from the Amplified® Bible (AMP), Copyright © 2015 by The Lockman Foundation. Used by permission. www.lockman.org.

Scripture quotations taken from the Amplified® Bible (AMPC), Copyright © 1954, 1958, 1962, 1964, 1965, 1987 by The Lockman Foundation Used by permission. www.lockman.org.

Scripture is taken from GOD'S WORD®, (GW) © 1995 God's Word to the Nations. Used by permission of God's Word Mission Society.

Scripture quotations taken from The Holy Bible, International Children's Bible® (ICB), Copyright© 1986, 1988, 1999, 2015 by Tommy Nelson™, a division of Thomas Nelson. Thomas

Can You Help?

I appreciate feedback, and I love hearing what readers have to say. Your input helps to make subsequent versions of this book and future books better. Please leave an honest review on Amazon letting me know what you thought of the book. Share your favorite quote or share a photo or video.

There's a whole community praying for God's healing hand to touch every reader, and we'd love to praise the Lord with you to celebrate your victory! If you have a testimony of healing, please email FirebrandUnited@gmail.com. Signing up for our free Healing Scriptures PDF at www.SallieDawkins.com will also allow you to receive early notification of new resources.

Thanks so much!

Sallie Dawkins

About the Author

Sallie Dawkins is a teacher, entrepreneur, and author with a powerful testimony of God's faithful love! She is passionate about seeing people healed and set free to enjoy abundant life in Christ.

A heart encounter with God in 2015 challenged Sallie's entire belief system. It was the beginning of the end of two-and-a-half decades of wavering faith and started her on a supernatural journey of discovery that rapidly transformed her life.

Sallie believes cultivating a deeper relationship with Jesus brought triumph over decades-long chronic pain and set her free from the frustration, doubt, and defeat of living under the influence of the enemy's lies.

This life-changing experience launched Sallie into ministry as an ordained Christian Healing Evangelist and Spiritual Coach. She loves to challenge Christians to know God intimately so they, too, can live in victory. Teaching through testimony, Sallie answers questions Christians can't, don't, or won't ask in church. Her three-part Awakening Christian Series is a valuable tool for guiding believers into a more meaningful relationship with God.

In 2018, Sallie Dawkins co-founded Firebrand United, LLC. Their products and services inspire and equip Christians to cultivate a deeper relationship with God.

Sallie lives in Kentucky, USA. Learn more at www.SallieDawkins.com.

About This Series

Many within the Body of Christ seem content with casual Christianity. The days of lukewarm, half-hearted Christianity must end if our goal is to grow in spiritual maturity. Have you ever dared to ask or believe that there might be more—*now*—on this side of Heaven? More that we don't have to wait to access? More of *something* on which you just can't quite put your finger? That's how Sallie Dawkins felt. She was no longer satisfied with living a complacent or powerless life as a Christian. She had a holy hunger for more. And the Lord answered that desire.

A heart encounter with God in 2015 challenged Sallie Dawkins' entire belief system. It was the beginning of the end of two-and-a-half decades of wavering faith and started her on a supernatural journey of discovery that rapidly transformed her life. Now an ordained Christian healing evangelist and spiritual coach, Sallie teaches through testimony, inviting born-again Christians to confront assumptions, doubts, and lies.

The three-part Awakening Christian Series is a valuable tool for guiding believers into a more meaningful relationship with God and answers questions Christians can't, don't, or won't ask in church. If we don't know or believe that God is who He says He is, how will we ever know or receive the fullness of His love for us? And if we cannot love ourselves and who we are in Christ, how will we love others as they deserve to be loved?

The lessons Sallie shares about her journey of spiritual growth can benefit every born-again Christian. This series is suitable for individuals and small groups. Readers will find valuable resources and application questions at the end of each chapter. Sallie Dawkins will show you how God brought healing to her own life, and how He can do it for you, too!

Book One of The Awakening Christian Series

Is God speaking to me?

Most Christians know God speaks through His Word, but when He speaks through the spiritual senses of sight, sound, touch, taste, and smell, it can leave a person feeling crazy! In **You Can Hear the Voice of God Through All Your Spiritual Senses**, Sallie Dawkins shares how she came to her senses in Christ in more ways than one! This book will help you to:

- Discover your true identity as a child of God

- Grow in awareness of God's presence as you navigate the supernatural awakening of your spiritual senses—*and it doesn't mean you're crazy*

- Recognize the voice of God over the other voices vying for your attention

- Grow in confident faith even after years of doubt and unbelief

- Restore peace, clarity, and freedom to your life as you learn to harness negative thought patterns

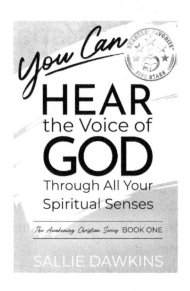

I'm impressed with how the author, Sallie Dawkins, gives her testimony. Her eloquence speaks to the reader, her writing shows glowing heartwarming honesty and humor. Incredibly intuitive, Ms. Dawkins teaches us how to experience God's incredible love through faith and belief. A must-read for those who long for and are seeking more from their relationship with Christ. It is a powerful read and a splendid and uplifting tool for those who wish to enhance their spiritual lives. – Susan S. for Readers' Favorite, 5/5 Stars for *You Can Hear the Voice of God Through All Your Spiritual Senses*

Book Two of The Awakening Christian Series

Is it possible to know God's heart?

In *You Can Know the Heart of God For Your Life,* readers continue their spiritual journey of transformation to grow in the image and likeness of God and will learn to:

- Seek God's will and view circumstances from Heaven's perspective
- Align with Jesus as the true Head of the Body to speak words of life and truth
- Unlock the soul-healing power of communion
- Restore peace to every area of life and allow that peace to shift atmospheres
- Grow in and benefit from the supernatural gift of discerning of spirits

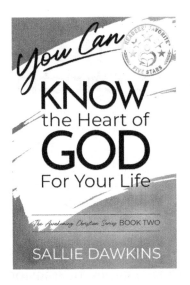

Every good Christian needs God in their life. Yet, how many have had the opportunity to be guided by an expert in listening to God's voice? That is why Sallie Dawkins' second book of The Awakening Christian Series, *You Can Know the Heart of God For Your Life*, is worth reading. In this inspiring volume, Dawkins recounts her experiences and offers them to you as a guide. I hope all readers who want God in their lives will take the opportunity to read a great book like this one. I think we all need it. – Astrid I. for Reader's Favorite, 5/5 Stars

Book Three of The Awakening Christian Series

Is God's healing power for me?

Can every believer access God's healing power, or is that reserved for an elite few? In *You Can Share the Love of God With Others*, readers are invited to glean from the author's journey of seeking truth that brings transformation to:

- Understand what it means to work out your salvation daily
- Practice basic spiritual authority, learning to call on the name of Jesus and apply the blood of Jesus over situations and circumstances
- Know and grow in your true identity as a born-again Christian
- Walk in Christ's authority and Holy Spirit's power to see others healed
- Learn practical tips for partnering with God and Heaven to fulfill the Great Commission

Simply put, *You Can Share the Love of God WIth Others* is an uplifting read for those in need of spiritual recollection. Sallie Dawkins writes in such a reassuring manner that her personal accounts of healing and receiving God's grace encourage you to shun your laziness in growing with Him. This is a spiritual guide that hooks you into its call to action. Part of the fullness of our spiritual maturity is answering to His call, in the same way that Jesus called for Peter to make it his life's mission to strengthen his brothers and feed God's sheep (John 21:17 NJKV). Read it, feel it, and live it. - Vincent D. for Readers' Favorite

Made in the USA
Middletown, DE
31 December 2021

57381870R00126